TECHNICAL EDUCATION

Technical Education

H.D. Kamat

A. David

CRESCENT
PUBLISHING CORPORATION

[The responsibility for the facts stated, conclusions reached and plagiarism, if any, in this book is entirely that of the Author. And the Publisher bears no responsibility for them, whatsoever.]

Technical Education

First Published : **2017**

ISBN 81-8342-041-9

Published by :

CRESCENT PUBLISHING CORPORATION
4831/24, Prahlad Street,
Ansari Road, Darya Ganj,
New Delhi - 110002
Ph. : 23272541, 23257835
Fax : 91- 011- 23257835
e-mail : campusbooks@hotmail.com

Typesetting by :

Arjun Computers
Delhi - 110051

Printed at :
Roshan Offset Printers
Delhi

PREFACE

Technical Education is an integrated, experience-based instructional programme designed to prepare students to be knowledgeable about technology—its evolution, systems, technologies, utilization, and social and cultural significance. It results in the application of mathematics and science concepts to technological systems in areas such as, but not limited to : construction, manufacturing, communications, transportation, biotechnology, and power and energy. Students are challenged to discover, create, solve problems, and construct solutions by using a variety of tools, machines, computer systems, materials, processes and technological systems.

Existance of polytechnics and other similar institutions all over the country offering a wide range of technical and skill-based career development courses such as gems and jewellery, footwear technology, plastics, food processing and construction management. There are hundreds of certificate and diploma courses available today which will suit any student and there are hundreds of institutions every where conducting short and long term courses.

Thus, technical education is a fundamental curriculum for all students, regardless of learning levels, career choices, or life aspirations. Students graduate from high school with the understanding of how technology affects daily decision-making; with the ability to use processes and systems, along with a variety of tools and resources to solve problems; and with the ability to apply and interrelate concepts in science, mathematics, language arts, and social studies to address practical issues in a technological society. Technology education teaches the concepts of tomorrow that enable students to turn their vision into reality today.

Contents

1

Education and Training in the Future

The Lessons of Experience

Until the end of last year, I was head of Sheffield City Polytechnic. The oldest constituent college within that Polytechnic is the Sheffield School of Art, which was established in 1842 to give apprentices, particularly in the cutlery industry, a firm grounding in the skills of their trade. When that school was founded, and indeed for a good number of years afterwards, our Victorian forefathers had no doubt whatever that the skills they were reaching those young boys were skills for a lifetime. They were skills meant to carry them through a whole working life, and neither the teachers, nor the governors, not those young lads of 13 or 14 themselves doubted it. This is the first point I want to make, because we know quite well that this is no longer true of any area of skills that we teach.

My second observation is also related to the Sheffield steel industry. This is a high technology industry and has been so for a very long time indeed. In Sheffield, they boast of selling steel by the pound rather than by the ton, and it is quite true because what they produce is all high alloy metal. But this is a high technology industry which is now under threat and having to struggle desperately to survive. The point I want to make here is that the fare of the Sheffield steel industry is by no means entirely determined by world trends, or anything of that sort. What is happening is rather the proof that any mature technology is a threatened technology, unless it continues to move with the times. Either things continue to change, and there is substantial continuing investment in new plant, new skills and new processes, or else . . .What we are seeing in Sheffield, with all its social consequences, is the 'or else' part of it.

My third observation takes me back to the time when I was a chemist. At that time, I went to do some post-doctoral work in the States, where there was a centre with an international reputation in the field. I was interested in. I was a member there of a team of about six, headed by a Fellow of the Royal Society of international renown, and supported by a team of very highly skilled technicians with a range of superlative equipment. The techniques we were using were then right at the forefront of knowledge, and it was a great privilege to be part of that team. But those same techniques are now performed by young school-leavers given a couple of days' training, if that. What is more, the level of their performance and their use of the techniques would put my efforts when I was doing post-doctoral work absolutely in the shade. That is how fast techniques can move from being in the forefront of knowledge to becoming a regular, routine part of industrial production. And that is the sort of speed of change that the new technologies are bringing into every part of our lives.

Now, every one of us could probably think of similar experiences in our own lives. I think it is important that we should reflect on our own past experience in this way, and then project that forwards and try to think what might happen over the next 20 or 25 years.

The Lessons of History

But outside our own lives, the lessons of history in the broader sense are also extremely valuable. What happened, for instance, as the industrial revolution got under way? It's an enormous question. But certainly one thing happened, or rather did not for quite a long time: the time lag between the economic, industrial and social changes of the industrial revolution and the consequent changes in education and training were absolutely enormous. And education and training only *responded* to economic, industrial and social changes: they did not *cause* them.

So much is perhaps obvious. However, there are two points I want to make about it. One is that education and training in this country never did catch up completely, and that the time lag for them to do so even partially was very much greater than in any other industrialised country. I suppose it could be said that things didn't really begin to change significantly in the wake of the industrial revolution until the physical communication system, the movement of people and goods, changed. That seemed to be the key to a whole lot of things that began to change very rapidly during the Victorian era.

The Victorian era can, I think, be regarded as the period of greatest change that this country has ever known, at least until very recently, and it is natural to look back to it in this context. In going so, however, there are factors we should bear in mind. First, all the changes of Victorian times came in on the back of a rapidly growing gross domestic product, and that is something we certainly do not have today. The changes we must bring about now have to be carried by a stable or even decreasing GDP. And second, we should realise that in Victorian times the infrastructure of the country-education, transport, all the services provided now by local government - was poorly developed. In fact, it was just being developed at the very time when all those changes in industry and in society were taking place. We find ourselves in a very different position. If we want to bring about change, we have to demolish the very infrastructure that we have and demolish is the word, because if we merely tinker with them we may find ourselves in a pretty desperate and disastrous situation.

A third factor we should bear in mind when we look back is that the economic and industrial changes that were taking place during the Victorian era were essentially for labour-intensive developments. Everyone wanted more and more labour. That, as we well know, is the reverse of the present case, so our response to change now has to be radically different from the Victorians.

Finally, we should bear in mind that countries that were first in the field in the early nineteenth century had things very much their own way. There was a certain measure of competition between the 'advanced' countries, but beyond that the world was their oyster. Now, of course, we can no longer depend on the buffer on reservoir of colonialism. To that extent, our position is quite different.

The Future

So much for looking back. Now I want to try to look forward, or perhaps even look at where we are at the moment. I am not going to attempt an extensive futurology because I think it would be quite pointless, and I won't and indeed I cannot propose specific remedies to specific problems because I don't think that that would help us in thinking through the parameters of change that we have to be aware of.

I want to start with the latest forecasts from the Warwick manpower model. I think this gives some helpful indicators, although many people may consider them rather vague. The Warwick model says that over the 20-year period from 1970 to 1990 there will be a 30 per cent reduction in the lower-level industrial skills (equivalent to about 2 million jobs lost), a 25 per cent reduction in craft and supervisory skills (1 million jobs lost), a 20 per cent *increase* in demand at the management and administrative level, and about 35 - 40 per cent increase in demand for higher-level industrial and service skills.

It is difficult to translate these projections into precise skills that may be needed over the next 10 years, but one or two things do stand out. (In fact, they have stood out for quite a long time, but unfortunately we haven't shown ourselves very responsive to the indicators.) The first thing is that, whatever we make of the total size of the labour force, certainly more skilled people are needed. That was become virtually a truism in the last 10 years, but how far has the education and training system responded to the obvious demand? Patchily so far, and that is why we need now to think what skills are and will be needed, and how we can teach them. The second point about the Warwick model (and about our experience of the labour market generally over the last 10 years) is that the skills we need are flexible, transferable skills. We need more people who can take skills from one job to another or from one industry to another, and who can build upon and change their skills in response to demand.

This whole concept of flexible skills challenge our education and training structures to the core, yet we all talk glibly about such skills, and we all go back to whatever we do in education and training and carry on very much as before, just tinkering with things as the margin.

There is one other thing we need to understand, which is not relaxed to skills at all, but is related to world economic trends: that we shall have to face more and more intense world competition. This will favour the highly developed nations, ourselves among them, provided we capitalise on our position and make sure we have the skills and knowledge necessary to compete in world markets.

There are two more points I want to make about forecasts of labour trends. First, there will have to be greater mobility of labour in all senses mobility between jobs, industries, careers, skills and geographical regions. And second, there must be more updating and retraining of the existing workforce, to renew and improve skills. I think this is clear from what has happened over the last 10 years. As I try to look ahead over the next 10 or 20 years, it seems to me that there are three things to note and to respond to. There is very strong evidence of a potentially serious shortage of top quality engineers for the next decade, and some evidence of a 15 per cent short fall in the supply of electronic, computer and software engineers by the year 2000. The danger of this, I think, is that a shortage of top quality people of this type will lose us our competitive edge in world markets and with it our chances of not only surviving in a more intensely competitive world, but actually rising somewhere near to the top of it.

This potential short-fall in top quality engineers has intriguing implications for salaries, too. Some statistical methods suggest that a 5 per cent shortage in any particular skill that is in demand produces within about five years a doubling of wages or salaries for those possessing that skill. So what will a 15 per cent shortage in top quality engineers do to the salary structures of that profession? And what then are the implications for the education system as a whole?

But, more importantly, it seems to me that the forecasts of labour trends show an urgent need to restructure employment.

We have to stop talking about this, and get on with it. If we don't, the social consequences are likely to be enormously disruptive. We are still nowhere near moving from the 50-50-50 structure for employment (in terms of years, weeks and hours) to a 40-40-40 structure, and I should have thought that in order to sustain economic and social stability we have got to move to 30-30-30 within 10 years. The political implications of this are so huge that, so far as I am aware, no political party is prepared to discuss it even superficially, let alone to think in terms of manifesto commitments. But we have to do it.

Lastly, a better skilled workforce has to mean a better educated workforce; and a better educated workforce will demand better information about the job it is doing, the markets it works in, and its own organisational structures within the company or firm. This is not a plea for participation, though I might argue for that elsewhere. I am merely pointing to something which I do not think has yet been recognised as clearly as it ought to be. The demand for more and better information and communication, which I think we can see already developing and which is bound to develop in the future, will place increasing demands upon the quality of management within firms and organisations. Therefore, management training and development will be crucial, alongside the training needed in other areas of skills.

Now, against this background of general manpower forecasting and general comments on the education and training response, I would like to point to the need for change in six areas.

1. *Local Responses to Local Needs*

The first I would describe as 'local responses to local needs". This may not seem to have much to do with the subject of this discussion, but I think it does, because it concerns the sorts of structure we shall be developing over the next 10 or 15 years.

There are signs, both in this country and all over Europe, of strong local and regional responses to local and regional conditions, in Merseyside, in Coventry, in the regions of France, and in the German Lander, it is clear that whatever national priorities and structures may exist, things are really happening at the local and regional level. If they did not, physical, material and moral depression would increase in those areas.

What is being created in all these places are new types of involvement for education and training in the industrial and business life of each area, and that involvement is backed up with facilities drawn from a range of support services. May be at the moment these are little more than gropings for local and regional initiatives and responses, but I think they are signposts for the future. These are grass-roots responses. Their effect at local and regional level is to blur or to break down the interfaces which until very recently have determined our education and training structures. Take, for instance, the interface between primary, secondary and further education. Here in Scotland, those interfaces are already breaking down, and will perhaps break down much quicker than elsewhere in Britain; but they are still there, and have done in my view a great deal to hinder curriculum and structural response. Another interface which is disappearing is that between vocational and non-vocational education. This is certainly not simply a result of the MSC's vocational education initiative, and here in Scotland the new 16 - 18 package is showing quite clearly that the interfaces and boundaries of the past will have to go.

Interestingly, also, there seems to be a growing awareness of the significance of the local education authority. Some have been saying for years in England and Wales that the Department of Education and Science was dead, but we should also have noticed (in England and Wales at least) that local education authorities have had one foot in the grave. Now suddenly, however, there seems to be a resurgence of interest in what the local education authority can do and wants to do in terms of its total provision. Instead of being the guardians of existing structures and systems, as for so long, the authorities are now beginning to ask questions about relationships between education and training, between the educational and industrial development strategies of the local authority; and between social change and the provision of education in the community. They are also asking very serious questions about the basis within education for the skills needed for the workforce in a particular area. I have put the question of local response to local need at the top of my list because I think it will be particularly important to the structures of education.

2. *A New Map of Knowledge*

My second area concerns the new map of knowledge which I believe the demands of the new technologies require us to draw. I have several reasons for thinking this. For one thing, I am convinced that our current examination system militates against education, particularly at secondary level, rather than encouraging it. It does not, at least, encourage the sort of education that would sustain change and the development of change. What a student is taught is conditioned to a large extent by the examination system, so that system really ought to reflect the map of knowledge that we need. If we are looking for more flexible skills and greater mobility, some of the boundaries which now exist almost solely to support the present education and examination system need to be redrawn.

The main impact of the new technologies on the curriculum and the map of knowledge, I think, will be a new emphasis on powers of synthesis as much as, and perhaps more than, powers of intellectual analysis. The consequences of this for our current curriculum structure will be expensive. A second implication will be a demand on a whole range of people, not only the most able, to deal with systems rather than with discrete entities. Again, the consequences for the curriculum will be very challenging indeed. I would say that at the moment our educational and examination system, and the structure of our present map of knowledge, probably require thinking in systems terms from only a tiny proportion of the population - perhaps 5 or 10 per cent. I think that very shortly we will need at least 40 per cent of the population to be able to think in those terms. There are enormous consequences here for the intellectual skills we seek to develop in young people as they go through the educational system.

A third effect of the new technologies will undoubtedly be to create a growing requirement for more and more people at work to communicate effectively. I don't think we have taken the measure of this yet. Increasingly, as we talk about communications, we should be dealing with the whole gamut of communication systems. The highly specialised and tremendously sophisticated systems currently being used in some areas will become the general property of a whole range of workforce. We must decide how to encourage the use of these systems and how to provide the skills necessary for their use. I doubt whether English literature as presently taught is the answer.

The final effect of the new technologies that seems to me to point to a need for a new map of knowledge, is the creation of a new attitude towards change. We need to welcome change rather than suspect and fear it, or seek to avoid its consequences. It is not only the trade unions that resist change: there is a considerable resistance inherent in our educational structures and in the map of knowledge that we project to young people and continue to live with even in higher education.

So we need to begin to tackle the job of drawing a new map of knowledge. I support that we shall have to start by grasping the nettle of what we mean by 'vocational'. Certainly, we can no longer simply mean something job-related. That has to go. But what do we mean? How do we create a vocational education that prepares somebody for 30 years of working life with not only many changes of job, but also perhaps two or three changes in career?

3. *Systems and Diagnostic Skills*

I mentioned earlier the need for higher-level skills, and here I see two areas of particular need. We need, quite specifically, to produce more people with higher skills who will be capable of designing, using and adapting systems of almost biological complexity. That need, I think, is going to be crucial. I think it will involve many more people than the few specialists in electronics and computers that we normally think of in this context.

The band of people needed to design and adapt systems of that complexity will be very considerable in 10 years' time. How are we going to produce the numbers, and the quality? We certainly need a sustained and massive training programme for teachers and trainers in the first place, and that will take a lot of resources.

At a second level, still with high but not absolutely top-level skills in the design and adaptation of systems, there will be a growing need for high-level technicians. A few years ago people were saying that every professional engineer needed four or five supporting technicians. I don't think that was ever quite true; in electronics today I suppose every professional engineer needs about half a technician. Of course, people think that technicians doing essentially diagnostic jobs can automatically be replaced by a microchip. It is not necessarily so. I believe to the contrary that we need to respond to the new technologies in relation to the education and training of high-level technicians by placing greater emphasis upon developing diagnostic skills and by being willing to see those skills change quite rapidly over time. We are not at present very good, particularly within education, at reaching diagnostic skills. Moreover, the general application of even the existing technology within industry will mean pretty rapid and massive changes within the technician workforce and the generality of mechanical and production and manufacturing engineering and industry over the next 10 years or sooner. It has happened already in the electronics industries in the last five years or so. Technicians will need greater adaptability, more highly developed diagnostic skills, and a greater willingness to change those skills.

4. *Adult Education*

We also need to think about more and better education for mature adults. It is a familiar plea but bears repeating, because the need for updating, re-skilling and retraining is absolutely vital. Unfortunately, our current structures within education and training are just not designed to meet these needs. Admittedly, if you go into the average college of further education or polytechnic or university, you will find interesting things happening in post-experience or post-qualification education, but it is likely to be fairly marginal to the general disposition of resources within the college.

As for training systems within industry, they are governed by the front-end loading system and are moving only very slowly towards a continuous input of updating and retraining modules.

If we move substantially into education for mature adults, therefore, there will be extensive consequences for the very structures both of our colleges and of training within industry. I don't want to start beating the drum for open and distance learning or the Open Tech but these are certainly possibilities to help us meet the need for change within the structures of education and training.

One great benefit from providing more and better education for mature adults is still. I think, not fully recognised. This is the reduction in lead time. The lead time we generally accept within education is very long indeed. For degree courses, the lead time from registration of a student to effective performance is probably about 10 years. Further back in the education system, the lead time for the consequences and impact of educational change is even longer than that. The point about more and better education for mature adults is that it very significantly reduces the lead time for responding to change. Increasingly, companies want skills today, or more realistically in six months' time: two, three or five years hence just will not do. So it is a very important point that the more we can provide opportunities for educating mature adults, the more we can reduce the response time of the education system.

Even at the professional level, the demand for updating is likely to increase. There is evidence recently of a number of professional bodies beginning to insist on what in Canada is called 'punitive education': a professionally qualified person who wants to retain recognition must be updated or else. I think this demand for relevant updating at the professional level will increase substantially and quite fast.

5. *Educational Technology*

We have to think about educational technology. However, we defined it, I would say that educational technology is at present not generally regarded as being central to the educational process. If we are to meet changing needs for better skills in the workforce, it is essential that educational technology should become central to the educative process. Otherwise, we shall not be able to deliver. The consequences of this are profound. To many teachers accustomed to chalk and talk they will seem mind-blowing, because ultimately the consequences will be to require a complete change in status of the learner and the teacher. It is as profound as that. No matter what skills are needed in the workforce. I think the delivery systems that we shall have to develop within education will require an acceptance of educational technology on a scale that up to now few people have envisaged.

6. *Staff Retraining*

The last point I want to make, drawing a number of these threads together, is that they all point to an absolutely paramount need for a sustained effort in staff development and training. I am not aware at the moment of a commitment in the education system to any such programme sufficient to meet the new demands that will be placed upon teachers over the next 10 years. Some of these demands are obvious. Teaching staff in schools, colleges, polytechnics and universities, for instance, will all need to be updated. At the moment, in any average engineering department in tertiary education, some of the staff will present a collection of obsolescent skills, completely out of touch with recent advances in industry and technology. The same is true of a number of other areas of knowledge that have moved on very quickly. Equally, trainers in industry need to have their skills updated. A particular danger, however, is that we may in some areas not possess the knowledge within the country to train and update our teachers and trainers. There are substantial parts of manufacturing industry in this country whose machinery is being produced wholly or mainly abroad. I think it is clear, therefore, that a substantial updating programme for teachers and trainers is needed pretty quickly, but that training material may have to be imported to do it.

I think that teachers and trainers will also need help in adapting their teaching skills to meet the needs of mature adults. These needs are not the same as those of initial trainees. In particular, teachers will have to learn to give up the centre of the stage to the learner. There will have to be a process of negotiation between learner and teacher, and teachers will need counselling and guidance skills in good measure.

It will, I think, be necessary for people in education to receive adequate training, also, in what I can only call community involvement. This means involvement with industry in the area, as well as with the whole range of activities that go on out in the community. If skills and jobs are changing rapidly, we must no longer provide specific skills for specific jobs, but a range of skills grounded in the community, and we shall need the support of the community to do it.

Finally, I feel that teaching staff must be better trained in curriculum management. I believe teachers are generally poor at this. What I mean is not only updating syllabuses (although that is badly needed); I mean also the pruning of syllabuses. Any survey of learners, particularly of reasonably mature students in training, on what they have been taught, shows a general dissatisfaction with the quantity of material they have been given that they will never use. A survey like this landed on my desk only last week, and there was a common feeling in the responses that as much as 70 per cent of the material TEC syllabuses was redundant for those students. Curriculum management means reducing unnecessary content. It also means ensuring that the content of module A is sensible when set alongside module B, and that the whole course is coherent. This is important for improving cost-effectiveness in education and training, as well as for increasing student satisfaction.

It is, however, undeniable that we shall achieve none of the things I have mentioned and meet none of the demands of the new technologies unless we are prepared to devote greater resources to staff development. If we fail in this, then we shall not succeed in teaching the new skills and creating an adequate educational response to the needs of information technology.

DISCUSSION GROUP REPORTS

In this the conference members were put in groups of balanced interests, and specific questions about the likely effects of the new technologies in education and training were put to each group.

Question 1

How far will information technology affect the aims and the methodology of education and training?

(a) There was a strong tendency to assert that the aims of education would not be affected at all by developments in information technology. Doubt was expressed about the meaning of the term 'information technology', which was sometimes regarded as the same as 'educational technology'- a systematic approach to the solution of problems across the whole spectrum of education. Others defined IT as 'any technical means to create, store, transfer, access, present or disseminate information' and saw it usually as a means, relating to methodology and not to aims. Aims were then seen as subject mainly to changes deriving from societal or political pressure rather than technical advance.

(b) This view was questioned, but not always in matters relating only to aims. Predictions included the following:

(i) Since IT would affect society it would therefore inevitably affect aims in education.

(ii) The roles of teacher and pupil were likely to be so changed that education itself would be changed. IT might achieve this by diminishing the gap between teacher and learner: by altering present definitions of literacy and numeracy so profoundly that aims would be affected: or indirectly by making new kinds of information available to a wider learner population.

(iii) The teacher would become a resources manager and the new technologies would give fresh impetus to approaches like individualised learning. As a result, emphasis on pupil-independence would be strengthened, and impetus given to other affective aspects as well as to cognitive elements. The necessary changes in teacher attitudes would change the aims.

(iv) IT as a delivery system was perhaps purely methodological, but IT as a subject in itself would become important. Aims would alter because of a growing need to encourage a more selective and critical use of information.

(v) A creative use of IT would stimulate conversation and discussion as it had done in Special Education, and so alter teachers' targets.

(c) In terms of methodology, all groups recognised the importance of IT mainly in terms of the individualisation of learning or a shift to learner centred approaches.
One group distinguished between 'training' as 'the practical application of principles' and 'education' as 'the presentation of and learning about principles'. All other groups appeared to see this distinction as increasingly unnecessary.

(d) Doubts were expressed about the strength of political will to make the means of change available and about the ability of teachers to respond positively to the new challenge.

Question 2

What implication does IT have for the content of the curriculum?

(a) A minority felt that content would not change, but only the means of presentation.

(b) Most saw some likelihood of change, and probable changes were identified as:

(i) The addition to the curriculum of new elements like keyboard skills for all, data handling, and data processing; and an even greater emphasis than now on the importance of reading skills.

(ii) More time for individualised learning.

(iii) More time for the expressive arts and other creative pursuits, if learning became more efficient.

(iv) Blurring of subject boundaries, leading to a growth of genuine interdisciplinary studies, involving a problem-solving approach.

(v) Pruning of the present curriculum (some were unhappy about who might carry this out), because rapid access to information would reduce the need for individual knowledge.

(vi) Greater individual choice: as students learned to use information, they would increasingly identify their own learning paths. The curriculum would become a flexible and adaptable menu of opportunities.

(vii) New methods of (external) assessment to meet and also to promote the new developments.

(viii) The evolution of a new 'classical' education, e.g. the learning of logic through writing programmes.

(ix) A 'negotiated day' becoming more practicable with a greater degree of individualised learning.

(x) Easier access to areas of the curriculum once considered 'difficult', e.g. numerical analysis in geography, for less numerate students.

Question 3

What will be the role(s) of face-to-face contact in the new situation?

(a) Most recognised continuing values for face-to-face contact, on a variety of grounds:

(i) Change should be 'evolutionary, not revolutionary'. There should be no sudden departures from present norms.

(ii) More individual contact, not less, would be possible, and should be used.

(iii) Human contact was needed for developing inter-personal skills, self-esteem, many types of group learning or team approaches to problem-solving, and respect for the human intellect, as well as for providing immediate human feedback.

(iv) It was felt highly undesirable to create the 'isolated individual learner'.

(b) The new emphasis on 'discussion' rather than 'exposition' would be more demanding for teachers, and necessitate changes in pre-service training. In-service support would be needed for all interactive approaches. The new pupil-teacher 'talk-situations' would be much more varied and open-ended than they often were now, since they would more often be initiated by the pupil. Teachers needed to be trained also to exploit the new technologies so as to give them time to use in other ways.

Question 4

What (new) skills and attitudes will be required in the learners and from the learning processes?

(a) In the pupil. The groups stressed the need for:

- (i) More responsibility, more self-discipline, and more control of the learning situation. There should be autonomy and self-direction in learning but, at the same time, an ability to co-operate with peers.
- (ii) Enquiring attitudes, abilities to synthesise, and divergent thinking. Learners would have to be less passive.
- (iii) The old skills in reading, study, manual dexterity, concentrated thinking, and referencing, used in a new way for sifting, selecting and evaluating information.
- (iv) New skills like keyboard operating and possibly programming (with a new respect for accuracy).
- (v) New attitudes to life-long learning, and flexible attitudes to different situation, probably of an open learning type.

(b) In the teacher. The groups identified the need for:

- (i) More adaptability and flexibility.
- (ii) An increased drive to motivate pupils, and place 'guided learning' alongside 'computer-assisted learning'.
- (iii) Willingness to acquire the strategies to develop learners' ability to pursue their own learning. Primary teachers were alleged to be better at this than those in secondary or further education institutions.

Question 5

What are the implications for institutions, firms and administrators in terms of accommodation, work patterns, organisation and management, and resources planning?

Most groups were running out of time by now, but knew that they would be taking up this topic again on a sector basis the following day. Many thought that there might be major changes if financial and other resources were made available, but most doubted that this would happen.

(a) There was general agreement amongst the groups that:

- (i) Traditional hierarchical structures might change because information would be more available at all levels, leading to greater decentralisation and democratisation.
- (ii) School design would depart from "corridors and boxes', and more small areas would be created.
- (iii) IT might become a management tool, and computer-managed instruction might develop, as distinct from computer-assisted learning.
- (iv) Local authorities might not be able to meet the financial demands or cope administratively with the rate of change.

(b) More random assertions included the following:

- (i) Yearly accounting made forward planning difficult, so more powers of virement would have to be given to institutions by funding bodies so that they could be more flexible and responsive to change.
- (ii) At present, change was inhibited by the amount of money tied up in obsolete equipment.
- (iii) The education system generally was not geared to the present rate of change.
- (iv) The present concepts of school or college day and year might have to be abandoned.
- (v) Courses would become much more skills-orientated than subject-content-based.
- (vi) More change would be needed in course providers' and teachers' attitudes than in institutional structures or patterns where administrative and staffing restraints would operate.
- (vii) On the other hand, the moves to open learning systems, distance learning courses or Open Tech structures meant considerable readjustment.
- (viii) Modular course structures would be required as one outcome of a process of rationalisation and identification of common elements in courses.
- (ix) People needed to stop being afraid of IT as if it were a power in itself. It had to be seen as a human resource, and 'people should be educated as people'.

2

A New Prospectus

Change Follows Change

In the twelfth centrury, two new inventions became commonplace in Europe. The post windmill which turned to face the wind no matter from which direction it came tripled the work a mill could do each year, making it possible to pump clear land previously flooded. The almost simultaneous introduction of a rigid horse collar replacing the flexible harness in use since Roman times increased the drawing power of the animal by a factor of five. This made possible the cultivation of heavy soils previously inaccessible to arable farming and including those recently drained. Some have argued that it was the large increase in wealth consequent upon these two technical advances that gave rise to the Renaissance.

I do not expect you to accept that analysis at face value but it does illustrate a point. The reality of these two inventions is incontrovertible, as is their impact on agriculture, the dominant technology of those days. To asert that the increase in wealth necessarily and deterministically gave rise to the Renaissance is simplistic. The wealth might for example have been put to quite other uses. Yet it is very hard to dispute that such a major change in the bases of contemporary economy must have had a social and political consequence. In our present era it is clear that technical changes proceed at a pace incomparably faster. So fast does change follow change that we see a passing over of quantity into quality, to steal a phrase, and no longer is it enough to assume the future will be much like past periods of technical evolution, then seen a rapid. What we are facing has more the quality of a historic discontinuity than of a mere projection forward of what we already know.

The Thinking Machines

Let us consider some of the facts of our situation. To put the matter with the starkest brevity, we live in the age when the machines have begun to think. If these last words seem shocking, let us agree quickly that of course not all the range of human thought processes is yet available to them. Even so, these sentient machines already respond in complex ways to external stimuli including spoken human commands. They can speak intelligibly to us in their turn, calculate, make logical inferences and act upon them. They have the faculty of memory and are even capable, as yet to a limited degree, of learning. To deny the label of thought to what they do would be to crush the meaning of the word in the vice of an outmoded vitalism.

It is time to admit that yet one more conceptual barrier between creature and artifact has been destroyed and that it can never be reconstructed. There exit in the universe at least two kinds of intelligence and one of them is man-made. It is with this our social philosophy must come to terms. How has it happened, this incredible transformation in our perception of what is possible for the non-living? Earliest attempts at mechanising thought concentrated on arithmetic calculations. The idea of machines that will calculate is very old but in its earliest realisations did little more than give modest aid to human power. No purely mechanical device it seems has the potential to go far down this road. The transformation which has opened the door into the charmed garden of possibilities where we now find ourselves is the domain of electronics. It seems, even if it cannot be proved rigorously, that complexity of apparent response and behaviour in an artifact is only possible where there is great complexity of structure, as indeed in the brain.

Now, mechanical devices are made from parts independently fabricated and assembled together, usually by hand. Like the movements of a watch, they may seem miracles of complexity but in fact usually have only a few hundred parts at most. When the count of separable parts goes beyound the thousand mark, life becomes increasingly difficult for the mechanical engineer and great professionalism is needed to achieve products well adapted to their purpose and reliable in function. Our motor cars, of course, are in this class.

If we push the count of parts even higher, to 10 or 100,000 or even beyond 1 million, mechanical engineering has to accept defeat. Yet it is in precisely these realms of complexity and beyond that thought-like phenomena are observed.

Cost is also critical. If a million-part machine is to have social impact, it must be affordable by most people and this means that each of those million parts must cost less than a hundredth of a penny. In the mechanical domain nothing can be made for so little but today electronics can offer a circuit of such complexity even at that low price.

Fanally, there is the question of speed. Mechanical devices rarely respond in less than a thousandth of a second; a million devices interacting at this speed will respond but slowly to the call. Something enormously faster is desired. Put all of this together and it is clear that a mechanical thinking device is barely possible. With such technology, artificial intelligence is an unattainable dream. Electronics, however, can make it commonplace.

In the natural world, complex living cratures are not assembled but grow. Some have urged this path for our quest for the thinking machine, but destiny has not led us that way. Instead, our modern miracle is the child of the Victorian discovery, photography. William Henry Fox Talbot of Lacock invented photography in its modern form, but he was also the inventor of photolithography. Ordinary photographs are permanent visible images formed on specially sensitised paper. However, for pictures in books or magazines, printing blocks were needed. In photolithography, the image controls the etching of a metal block through a series of chemical processes. By inventing this technique, incidentally within only a few years of his first photographs, Fax Talbot did far more than democratise the photograph, significant though that was. Using the light-formed image to control etching, for the first time it became possible to fabricate artifacts by photographic means. Because microscopic images are easily formed by suitable optics, the door had opened to manufacturing things on the very smallest scale: the first step towards our contemporary microelectronics revolution.

The second step was the discovery of new electronic devices. Electronics began with the thermionic valve or tube which was invented by Lee De Forest and brought to perfection by Tellegan. Descended from the electric lamp it was large, fragile and very hungry of power. It had the necessary speed advantage over mechanical devices but in other respects its nature precluded it from being the kay to machine intelligence. Today, except for a few highly specialised niches, it survives only in modified form as the cathode ray tube of the television set. To be usable at the scale of complexity envisaged, what was needed was a device which could be very small, use negligible power, yet retain or surpass the speed of the valve. Such a device, today we call it a transistor, was invented in 1925 by Julius Lillienfeld of Leipzig. It was totally ignored. For the next two decades the transistor was repeatedly reinvented, yet failed to achieve recognition by the technical community.

Fanally, in the late 1940s John Bardeen and Walter Bratain is William Shockley's lab at Bell Telephone Laboratories invented the transistor yet again, but this time with such theoretical understanding and command of practical techniques that exploitation was feasible. The alchemy of time, place and people came right at last. For this achievement, the trio received the Nobel Prize, in Bardeen's case the first of two, but no other invention of the twentieth century is really in quite the same league as this one. Its long-term implication for the future of humankind invites the oft-made comparison with the invention of the wheel. That there were many precursors in no way detracts from the importance of this great advance; quite to the contrary, they demonstrate that the Bell researchers ultimately revealed what men of vision and technical virtuosity for a quarter of a century groped to find, just because they were able to see how critically formative such an advance would be. And they were right.

Today transistors are fabricated almost exclusively in an elemental crystalline solid called silicon. Derived from ordinary sand, silicon exists in two forms, p and n, which have quite different electrical properties but are distinguished only by the chemical characteristics of the minutely small traces of impurity which they contain. All of the electronic devices needed to make even the most complicated of circuits can be fabricated from suitably configured and juxtaposed regions of silicon. To complete the technical basis for microelectronics, therefore, all that was needed was some means to adapt Fox Talbot's photolithography to control the insertion of impurities into the silicon crystals - as simple as that.

Atalla and his associates had achieved this (again in the Bell Labs) by 1960, more than 20 years ago. Now at last it became possible to fabricate on the microscopic scale functional electronic devices capable of building up into circuits of biological complexity, yet all made at once by a single photographic process. The charge was laid, the fuse lit, nothing could stop the explosion of technology which followed.

The Silicon Revolution

Since the mid-1960s the practically attainable complexity of silicon microcircuits (silicon chips) has doubled about every 14 or 15 months and the cost per electronic function has halved in about the same period. Some of the consequences have been quite bizarre. For instance, in the mid-50s Ferranti produced its Pegasus computer. It cost then £50,000 which is something like half a million or so in modern money; it occupied a room larger than the average sitting room and made it very hot in summer; and was so fussy over its electricity supplies that it had to have its own motor generator. The machine was thought to be a prodigy of technology then and its users felt very privileged to get access to it. It was of course by modern standards an absolute brute to programme. Today I can carry a more powerful computer in my pocket. It costs about £100, runs for months on a little internal battery, and is so easy to programme that children enjoy doing it.

A technical change of this magnitude, widely applied, can end a historical epoch and inaugurate a new one. Yet this is not the end of the story; my personal computer is the product of what is only the half-way stage in the evolution of microelectronics, the changes go on and even accelerate. It is characteristic of a major technological advance that it inevitably tends to spread its influence far beyond the purpose for which it was originally evolved. Thus, is the great age of steam the pumping of water for which the steam engine was first invented became almost insignificant compared with the impact of steam locomotives and ships. The use of steam is the great motive power for agriculture, for industry and for the generation of electricity. Equally in microelectronics, an incomparably more significant technical advance has spread from the initial role of electronics in radio-communications into computers and robots and artificial intelligence and so on. In much humbler roles too, the reducing cost and increasing capabilities of microelectronics are enabling it to sweep out other technologies wherever it confronts them head on. Who could rationally prefer a mechanical wrist watch now when the electronic quartz watch looks the same, costs less and is 100 times more accurate. What of teleprinters and telephone exchanges and sewing machines and typewriters, once concatenated from fine springs and metal parts, but now inwardly motionless and silent, fallen under the perpetual sped of silicon? The ripples spread outward and outward. Even more familiar artifacts will be transformed as the tide of the new technology reaches them. Microelectronics, transforming all it touches, allows us to witness a rare social phenomenon, revolution uncorrupted by compromise, but a revolution drive only by a technical logic and innocent of any social purpose unless it be given one.

You will have heard those who argue that the new electronics will be used by the capitalists to strengthen their power and that of their class. No doubt they would if they could but they can neither understand nor bridle it any more than the rest of us. Others weave fantasies of a more darkly paranoid vein in which the new technology reinforces the oppressive power of a malign state, and so it might. Something so universal and so cheap as this could also just as well serve the interests of subversion, for all that we know. It is neither rational to dread the new electronics nor to trust it blindly. The best course for us is surely in coming to understand what the new electronics has to offer and trying to use it to achieve goals which, by some essentially political process, we have collectively chosen to pursue. Even this is simplistic. A knowledge of what is possible must surely influence what goals we set ourselves. As always in politics of a realistic kind, we iterate. What then are the social trends that the use of new technology already implies and what further possibilities yet to be clearly revealed ought to be introduced into the political debate? It is hard indeed to know where best to begin.

Will microelectronics, for example, increase or decrease the total available employment? Some say one thing, some another. Governments who realistically see no option but to encourage the new technology have a great emotional investment in asserting that, whatever the short-term problems, in the end employment must increase. In the past, so the legend runs, it has been feared that new technology would destroy employment and this will lead to Luddite violence, restrictive practices and what you will. The actual historical outcome has been quite different, and both prosperity and employment have benefited.

Unemployment - Loss or Liberation?

Technology has indeed improved general prosperity; this is hard to dispute, but as far as employment is concerned a closer look is required. It is at least plausible to argue that in the categories where industrialisation has destroyed employment, work has never returned. Agriculture is the pre-eminent example. There was a time when almost 90 per cent of the working population of these islands was employed directly or indirectly in agriculture. New that figure is under 5 per cent and falling still. The total agricultural product is at an all-time high. The same is true in other erstwhile labour-intensive industries. When the jobs are destroyed, they go for good. The expansion of trade alone will not bring them back again. By contrast, what does indeed transform the situation is the evolution of quite new kinds of jobs. But where this happens it is usually attributable to the recognition of new and different public or private needs which the available labour, displaced from other occupations, can satisfy with new goods and new services. In short, for a very long time we have habitually defined new categories of service as work, activities ranging from social care to professional tennis-playing, things that would not have been done at all in the past, or if done would have been seen as 'good works' or as a pastime, rather than as gainful employment.

Similarly, we now define as goods and go out and shop for things ranging from video-tape recorders to ethnic Peruvian woolly hats, which our forebears did not conceive of as articles of commerce or clothing. But let us not fool ourselves, no process of technological determination brought this about. We want social workers, those of us who still do, because we have expanded our concept of the duties of the state towards its citizens, and we support professional tennis-players because we have modified the received perception of recreation. Many people buy videorecorders because the same state has determined to deny them access to pornography over broadcast television channels. We purchase missiles to serve our expanded way of war and we choose Peruvian hats because they are fashionable and perhaps because we would like to help a less developed country - perhaps.

It is painfully obvious that, when all is said and done, it is social forces and not technology that determine employment levels. However, they do so in the context of a game, and the rules of that game the technologists are perpetually rewriting, but in a way that they cannot themselves articulate and nobody else fully understands. Since World War II, and despite Keynesian economic policy, British unemployment has risen pretty steadily with only minor fluctuations. To this pattern, the colour of the government of the day has been largely irrelevant. Evidently new kinds of employment have not been crated as fast as technical change has destroyed old kinds of work. The moral is clear, we face a political and social crisis, not a technological or really even an economic one. Above all, we must not seek refuge from our fears in the hope that new industries created by microelectronics will generate a host of new jobs. No labour-intensive activities are remotely in view from that quarter. Instead, labour will continue to be freed progressively from all kinds of manufac-turing as the thinking machines take over the role hitherto filled by the partnership of human intelligence and the more primitive insensate machine of the pre-electronic era.

Thus, for the major part of the population, manufacturing industry as we have hitherto known it will offer a rapidly diminishing employment opportunity. The social options most positive in this situation are an acceptance of less work, or the redefinition of human activities, new or old, as work where not at present so identified. It is potentially tragic that these problems present themselves when the international economic community is apparently hell-bent on policies which persuade many of us that we are too poor collectively to countenance social changes such as these, which alone would safeguard our future collective tranquility.

In the immediate post-war period, the general adoption of Keynesian economic measures produced remarkable prosperity in the western world, but at a price. The real purchasing power of our currency, which had fluctuated within only modest bounds since Cromwell's day, went into an exponential decline. We are now enjoying the solution to this problem: a world-wide return to economic classicism. Inflation is cured but at the cost of a reduction of world economic activities on a scale not seen since last such policies were applied.

Our present economic hardships derive from no change in world resources. They are therefore manifestly voluntary, self-inflicted through economic policy. It would be a pity if they created a psychological environment which rendered it impossible to do the sensible things which would enable us to exploit new technology without social dislocation. Certainly we cannot wait for the economists to find a new theoretical formulation to deliver prosperity and low inflation together. No man can tell by how many future Nobel Prizes that golden prospect is remote. What microelectronics clearly implies at this stage of its evolution is that all present human tasks which require only simple perceptions, judgements and responses, particularly where the whole pattern can be expressed as a set of explicit rules, can and will be taken over by the thinking machines. In part at least it is surely perverse not to see this as liberation. The fact is that to make society run it was hitherto vital to extract as much work as possible from its members. As a result, all kinds of mechanisms have been developed to encourage acquiescence in the highly unnatural business of working. Distribution of wealth through the wage mechanism is the most obvious. This is now partly breaking down; state welfare payments of various kinds play a not inconsiderable role in the distribution of wealth in most developed countries, with the exception of Japan. But the non-monetary incentives to work connected with powerful intangibles like social standing and self-esteem have as yet been little undermined. Perhaps one day we shall come to see the hippies and the flower people of the 1960s as premature prophets of a new social order. The prevailing economic sado-masochism makes it difficult just now to put forward such a view and be heard, except in Scotland - but there is worse to come.

The Engineering Elite

Were the forthcoming loss of jobs all that we had to worry about, to muddle through might yet be a reasonable hope, but the actual situation is even more challenging. Alongside a great reduction of employment for many, paradoxically there is also likely to be a severe and worsening shortage in certain categories. The scientific and technical people needed to run the new high-tech economy will be hard to find in adequate numbers. As the unskilled and semi-skilled are eliminated from the process of mass-production, only a little later the personnel of industry will increasingly become professionalised. The young graduate engineer, through computer-aided design and manufacture, is already today capable of commanding the production process directly, in many cases without further human mediation. In the extreme, by doing so, he may generate half a million pounds per year of added value by his own single-handed effort. This state of affairs must spread through almost all manufacture, and as it does so the professional engineer becomes the crucial factor in production. The availability of such people may be the determinant of the scale of economic activity at any future time.

This has some very interesting consequences. First, the number of people of this ilk will always remain quite small compared with the population as a whole. Very many people do not have the particular kind of talent required for this work and it is certain that the overwhelming majority do not have the inclination. The ugly word élite at this point forms in the liberal mind, yet it is important not to jump to unwarranted conclusions, for numerically small and economically vital groups within society do not always exercise inordinate power or enjoy great privileges, witness the case of agricultural workers. In a sense, the apparent élite of professional information technologists might rather be seen, like agricultural workers, as an underprivileged group. The engineers will work to sustain the rest of us and most of the value they create will have to be stolen away from them whether by taxation or by howsoever. It must be so, if the rest of us are to live. The microelectronics engineer becomes like a parody of the workers in the classical formulation of Marxism: in theory crating the wealth, but having most of it expropriated. The bizarre difference is that the exploiters and not the exploited will be overwhelmingly in the majority. We shall all be members of the boss class then, grinding the faces of the technically gifted. Evidently Marxism exemplifies the dictum that history always repeats itself, the first time as tragedy, the second time as farce.

For Britain, of all the nations, the future is particularly fraught. Relative to the size of our population, we produce one graduate engineer where Japan produces eight. This alone, if uncorrected, must mean that our economy levels off far lower than theirs; yet what chance have we of getting it right in a country in which it has in the past been common for politicians and public servants to consult distinguished scientists about national policy for technology? A perceived need for computer technologists may all too easily in consequence be translated into an increased output from the universities of radio-astronomers. The decades pass, fine words are spoken, and still effective reform eludes us. Our young people are no less talented than those of other nations. No law of science dictates for us the inevitable decline: we choose it, and we choose it again by our politics, our collective world view startlingly uniform from left to right of our political spectrum.

Innovate or Die

Many times in the past our country has saved itself, often when things looked hopeless. Can it do so again? Perhaps our children, taking to computers in their infant schools as once we took to bead frames, will in their time show us how it is done. May be our government in late day has at last perceived, like none before it, that innovation is our economic life and has found the courage to let old industries die so that new ones may come to birth. If only we in Britain could believe that we have found the collective will to take one quarter of what has been spent on prolonging unnaturally the existence of industries dead in all but name, and spend that money on promoting and cherishing the industries of our future. The Japanese, those vexing paragons, are reported ready to abandon shipbuilding to its commercial fate, yet spend money on their fifth generation computer project as if there were no tomorrow.

Yet, as I speak, fear forms that such a transformation could not be. What I have said is surely far too radical or perhaps too reactionary a thought, unmannerly, not in the decent British tradition that we love. I seem to hear my amiable compatriots saying that perhaps he is wrong after all, the microelectronics revolution might never happen, or if it does it may be that we shall somehow stumble through. If indeed it is written that gentle decline is the future of our country, that this is to be our response, then we must turn and turn and sleep again, dreaming our several dreams: some of the ever-rising FT indexes, green pheasant-haunted acres, and Harrods at Christmas; others of the workers' triumph, safe from the test of life by infinite postponement, in which the whole world will be one great co-op store and none will dare lift his head above his neighbour. Diverse dreams, perfectly interlocking yet touching at no point, lap against the feared cold. Sleep on then, if indeed we are an old people, stiff in the bones, who cannot and will not rise to meet the day. Yet that is not my conviction, for I believe that those sleepers slow to waken yet have it in their power to do great things. The signs point many ways, but there is a stirring in our country, a willingness at last to be enthusiastic for new technology. More computers are found in our schools than in those of other countries and 1982 was our year of information technology as well as of conflict in the Falklands.

In the smooth, veiled face of that loved and damnable English liberal consensus, a crack has appeared, and now grown to a chasm. The deep conservation of our people is challenged and we stand like men struck by news of great portent debating which way we should turn. Talk and talk on, for debate is the stuff of political process, but be warned: this is the age of the thinking machines and they will not be denied.

INFORMATION TECHNOLOGY IN EDUCATION AND TRAINING

Cause for Concern

I had better begin by acknowledging my limitations as a speaker on this theme. I am not an expert on the new technologies - indeed I know far too little about them - but their influence, present and potential, on our lives is so great that I am compelled, both as chairman of the CCC and as a headteacher, to consider their implications for the school curriculum. The economy, the Scottish economy especially, is becoming steadily more dependent upon them. Press coverage is constantly increasing. The government is very concerned. It has accepted the recommendations of the Alvey Committee on advanced information technology for a development programme costing £350m over five years. Following up one of the detailed recommendations of the Alvey Report the government, despite its commitment to retrenchment in higher education, has provided additional finance for 70 new information technology posts in the university sector alone, 30 primarily for research, 40 primarily for teaching, with 400 additional student places to accompany them. The world of work and the world of leisure are already profoundly affected by developments in information technology. Banking is revolutionised. Retail businesses with multiple outlets are introducing systems which will give them virtually instantaneous stock control. Twice this week *The Times* carried articles on the use of technology by the police in the fight against crime. Was it 400,000 personal computers sold at

Christmas? Our pupils are already adapting to the new technologies outside the school. What opinion will they of an education system which fails to take account of these developments?

What are the main categories of information technology with which we are concerned in education? They are, I think:

1. The by now fairly familiar field of audio-visual aids, expanded by developments in telecommunications.
2. Computing.
3. Office technology.

These three categories of information technology are perhaps unique in education in that each is both an end and a means, both a subject in its own right and a teaching or learning aid, and therefore both content and process.

IT as Content

Let us look at them first as subjects of study.

1. *Media education* is an area of the curriculum in which interest has been increasing recently. This is due to the enthusiasm of teachers - I understand that a recent conference on media education was attended by some 130 teachers - supported by the CCC in its short course development programme. Strictly, it is a multidisciplinary study; in practice, because multidisciplinary studies are difficult to organise on a school's tight timetable, courses are being developed mainly by teachers of English.

2. *Computing* first entered the school curriculum in the 60s. In 1967 the Secretary of State, on the advice of the CCC, set up the Computers and the School Committee under the chairmanship of Mr. A. T. Bellis, headmaster of Daniel Stewart's College, Edinburgh, to consider the implications of computers for the schools. In its Final Report, published as a Curriculum Paper in 1972, the Bellis Committee recommended that:

    (a) An introductory course in computer studies should be provided for the great majority of pupils. Teachers of various subjects should be encouraged to co-operate in presenting the course.

(b) Further work relating to computers should generally be incorporated into the teaching of the various school subjects.

(c) Computer studies should not be developed as a subject discipline in its own right.

Towards the end of the 70s, the CCC recognised that the pace of development in computing, the range of applications in society and the increasing availability of computers in schools made necessary some modification of these policies. The question of an O grade course in computing was remitted to a Joint Working Party of the CCC and the Scottish Examination Board, and this is now being piloted in a limited number of schools. To speed up other developments the CCC established in April 1981 a three-year project on microelectronics, computing and the curriculum with a project steering committee under the chairmanship of Professor J.K. Standley, Professor of Physics at the University of Dundee. The steering committee has just published a syllabus for computer appreciation in S1 and S2; it is working on guidelines for teachers planning a non-certificate course in S3 and S4; and it has various other projects in train in collaboration with certain education authorities and central committees of the CCC. The steering committee has identified inadequate provision of software as one of the main barriers to progress. Acting, to use Professor Standley's term, as a friendly irritant, it has managed to persuade government to allocate additional funds for this purpose, though not as much as it would like. Another question being raised at the moment is the speed of development of certificate courses. The new O grade course in computing will not be generally available until 1985 with the first certificate awards in 1987. Should this timetable be speeded up? At what stage should computing appear in the Munn Dunning Implementation Programme for the development of new credit, general and foundation courses? And should electronics, as distinct from computing, be developed as a school subject - a question raised by the Central Committee on Science?

3. *Office technology* is the third category of information technology which I identified earlier. It is not a separate subject in the school curriculum; but it is an important element of the business studies syllabus and an element which must constantly be updated to reflect current developments.

More generally, it should be said that there is a need to give a larger place to technology, that is the applications of knowledge, in the school curriculum. The CCC recognised this and has set up a Committee on Technology to advise it in this matter.

IT as Process

The other aspect of the new technologies I wish to discuss - in a conference organised by SCET it is perhaps the main aspect which should be discussed - is that of the teaching or learning aid. The potential in each of my three categories is very considerable.

1. *The audio-visual category* comprises the overhead projector, slide projector, film, television (much more useful now that the videorecorder is commonplace), radio, the tape recorder, charts, maps - the list could go on. By far the most common function of these aids is illustration; illustration is a more vivid, memorable and realistic manner than is generally possible by the spoken word. There are other functions, for example, the overhead projector is often used for summarising purposes; if my talk had been more factual and less reflective in its content, I should probably have used OHP transparencies. The tape recorder is useful for developing oral skills - particularly oral composition. Some of these aids grow more useful as they develop more sophisticated facilities - viewdata, for example, although it is as yet scarcely exploited for school use. Some grow less useful as curricular objectives change - the language laboratory is less important than it was 10 years ago in the teaching of modern languages, because of the stress now laid on communication competence, with pupils working in pairs or small groups rather than individually.
2. *The computer.* I am sure that I do not need to stress the importance of the computer as a teaching aid. I do not myself

know much about its detailed applications, although I understand from talking to teachers that among the more interesting is the testing of hypotheses and the following through of alternative assumptions, particularly in the social subjects.

3. *Office technology.* It may, however, be necessary to underline the importance of office technology. With so much of the work of curriculum development now falling where it properly belongs - on teachers in the schools - high quality reprographics are essential if teachers are to carry out their task of putting flesh on the bones of national guidelines and produce good teaching and learning materials. This increased professional commitment also makes greater demands on teachers' time and makes it more than ever necessary to free them as far as possible from routine chores by the introduction of computerised administration.

For convenience I have discussed my three broad categories of information technology individually, but this categorisation is, of course, largely artificial. They can be broken down and recombined in different ways. In their varying combinations they can be used to promote individualised learning. Learners proceed with their own studies, at their own pace. Individualised learning is a much favoured principle. Computer-directed learning (CDL) may considerably extend the possibilities in this field once the appropriate hard-and software become generally available.

The new technologies, then, have much gong for them. They are seen as an important new force in British industry. They are strongly supported by government. They appeal to pupils to a greater degree than some of the more traditional subjects, and this has led to the development of new elements in the school curriculum. They can be powerful aids to the processes of teaching and learning, including individualised learning.

The Answer for the 1980s?

So are they the answer to the educational problems of the 1980s? In my view they are part of the answer, but by no means the whole of it. In considering the school curriculum you start with aims and objectives, which relate mainly to the needs of the learners and of society; you move to a view of the curriculum as a whole and thence to a view of its individual components, whether these be subject disciplines of the traditional kind or multidisciplinary studies. I have tried to indicate how the curriculum is being affected by the new technologies - a growing interest in media education, computer appreciation courses for all, computer studies courses for pupils with a particular interest, elements of office technology within the business studies course, a growing recognition of the importance of technology generally.

From the curriculum you pass to methodology. Methodology can be defined as the principles and techniques of teaching. Now, teachers - teachers in schools, that is, not teacher-trainers - have tended in the past to think of methodology as secondary and to downgrade it. This is understandable - the message must be more important than the medium. Hence, there has been as excessive reliance on traditional expository methods - 'chalk and talk'. Successive inspectorate reports on different aspects of education have made the same criticism of teaching-sound but unimaginative.

Insofar as this statement relates to the exploitation of the new technologies, one must recognise that teachers have problems. There is the speed of change - educational development is normally a fairly slow process. There is the variety of inputs - from education authorities, from government, from quasi-governmental bodies such as SCET and the CCC. And the familiar in more comfortable.

There are some hopeful signs. In discussion of pedagogy, the art of teaching, I have the impression that the term 'methodology' is being used less frequently. It is gradually being replaced by the term 'process'. One can see why. The term 'methodology' is essentially teacher-centred. The term 'process' applies both to the process of teaching and the process of learning; and the first is important only insofar as it affects the second. Again, I believe that there is emerging a new breed of bright, young highly professional principal teachers. And schools are gradually developing the administrative structures to exploit that professionalism through committees on computing and educational technology. Educational planners at all levels are finding that the secret of curriculum development is to identify examples of success, sometimes through planned experiment, sometimes by discovering individual initiatives and building on these. This applies to the exploitation of education technology as to all else.

There is, however, a risk of overkill with the new technologies. The enthusiast may be tempted to identify microelectronic technology with education, to see in it the answer to all educational problems. There is a danger in playing with machines. One has constantly to ask oneself whether what one is doing is educationally valuable. Let me remind you again of the principles of curriculum planning. You start with aims and objectives, more thence to curriculum and then consider appropriate methodology. The new technologies, as I have attempted to show, have an increasingly important, but still limited, place in the curriculum. They have also an increasingly important, but still limited, place in methodology, in the processes of learning and teaching. Teaching and learning are as a general rule most effective where a variety of approaches are adopted. Now, educational technology can enrich expository teaching, it can enhance the possibilities of individualised learning. But there are other situations where it will have no role, or a lesser role, to play - discursive situations where the stress is on oral work in groups, guided to a greater or lesser extent by the teacher; or activity learning situations, where the stress is on children practising their skills in creative and practical activities. The 'language across the curriculum' committee in my school tell me that one of their main concerns is simply to provide children with more opportunities to talk. (They are, incidentally, planning to make a video with examples of good practice to encourage their more conservative colleagues, but have run into technical difficulties). When I talk with industrialists about the educational needs of industry, they complain that the schools fail to give youngsters the opportunity of learning how to co-operate in a task, to work together as a team. Now these oral and social skills need more attention than at present - and they are largely independent of educational technology; not wholly so; the tape recorder is a useful aid in the acquisition of oral skills. The fact is that in some teaching or learning situations the new technologies have an important role to play; in others a negligible role or none at all. They should be used when they aid the learning situation, not otherwise. They must not be allowed to take over.

There is one fairly new development which I should mention. Recently, curriculum planners have tended to play down the importance of content - witness reiterated demands in recent reports for the content of syllabuses to be pruned - and to give greater stress to process. They talk more of integrating content and process or at least of interweaving these two strands of learning. Now, educational technology is only a part of process, but I think that nonetheless this is a trend which should give encouragement to educational technologists.

Finally, what are the implications of the new technologies for colleges of education and for schools? I think teacher-trainers have to consider very carefully the applications of the new technologies in their own subject areas, taking account both of the thinking of curriculum committees and of their own assessment of the new developments. They have to take account of his new stress on the integration, or at least the closer association, of content and process - and that means seeing for themselves and not leaving it to the educational technologist or audio-visual specialist, that their students are equipped to exploit the new technologies. They should take advantage of the possibility, which the new technologies offer, of video-recording successful practice in the classroom and using that as a model in pre-service and in-service training. And they must find ways of making a bigger contribution to school-focused in-service training, perhaps through distance learning packages.

And the schools? I think they have to give what support they can to teachers, particularly probationary teachers. I discovered one the other day, a probationer, who could not use a film projector. Yes, she had been given instruction at college, but it was in the second year of her B.Ed. course and that was a long time ago. In my school we normally offer a short training course in audio-visual aids to probationers - I must make sure it has been laid on this year. The school must also provide the structure which enable enthusiasts in a particular field to come together and develop that enthusiasm, which will possibly rib off on others. As for the teachers, I am often consoled, as I look at the bleakness of some parts of the educational landscape, by the belief that there is a new professionalism among young teachers - perhaps because the colleges have been able to be more selective in recent years. That professionalism reveals itself most clearly in a willingness to take on board new developments.

DISCUSSION GROUP REPORTS

Sector Interest Groups

In this occasion the conference members were grouped in sector interests, as follows:

Group I	Local authorities - councillors, directorate, advisory staff.
Group II	A mixed group - schools, colleges of education, curriculum development, local authorities.
Group III	Industry and further education.
Group IV	Higher education other than colleges of education.
Group V	Schools, colleges of education and curriculum development.

Computerised Questionnire

All members had a digest of the previous day's discussions, and a computer analysis of answers given by members to certain questions on information technology on a machine installed in one of the exhibition areas. About 45 per cent conference members had given answers. Council staff, speakers, gorup leaders, recorders and so on were not involved in these responses, which were sought for interest, and not in any attempt to prove anything.

These were the questions, and the number of responses.

Question 1

Which of the following are, in your opinion, examples of information technology?

	Yes	*No*	*Don't know*
Broadcast television and radio	43	7	0
Computers	45	5	0
Video-cassette recorders	43	6	1
Telephone	33	17	0
Prestel	44	6	0
Calculators	24	25	1
Satellite television	43	6	1
Film projectors	29	20	1
Digital watches	23	26	1
Body scanners	40	10	0
Overhead projectors	30	20	0
Cash dispensers	29	21	0
Blackboards	29	21	0
Cable television	44	5	1

Question 2

As a result of the introduction of information technology into education and training, there may be a change in the number of teacher-trainers involved in the education system. Do you think that there will be:

	A an increase	B a decrease	C no change	in the number of teacher-trainers?
Answers:	25	13	11	

Question 3

As a result of the introduction of information technology into education and training, there may be a change in the number of education/training institutions. Do you think that there will be:

	A an increase	B a decrease	C no change	in the number of institutions?
Answers:	15	17	17	

Question 4

As a result of the introduction of information technology into education and training, there may be a change in the amount of face-to-face contact involved in the education/training process. Do you think that there will be:

	A	B	C	
	an increase	a decrease	no change	in the amount of face-to-face contact?
Answers:	14	29	6	

Question 5

Which of the following do you believe will happen as a result of the introduction of information technology in the home?

	Yes	*No*	*Don't know*
There will be a significant increase in the number of people who *learn* at home.	47	1	1
There will be a significant increase in the number of people who *work* at home.	40	7	2
The population as a whole will be better *informed.*	38	9	2
There will be a significant increase in the time people devote to *entertainment in* the home.	32	11	6

Question 6

In the 1990s, there may be a change in the use made of information technology in industry/commerce and in education/training. Do you think that industry/commerce will make:

	A	B	C	
	greater use	less use	comparable use	of IT in comparison with education/training?
Answers:	38	1	10	

Question 7

By the year 1990, there may be a change in the use made of information technology by learners in schools and in industrial/commercial training. Do you think that learners in schools will make:

	A	B	C	
	greater use	less use	comparable use	of IT in comparison with learners in industrial/commercial training?
Answer:	27	11	11	

Question 8

The part which young people leaving schools and going into industry/commerce in the year 1990 will play in the adoption of information technology in their place of work, will be:

	A	B	C
	significant	insignificant	don't know
Answers:	40	3	6

Group Discussions

The different sector groups were set different topics to discuss. Some overlap with the previous day in the topics chosen was both unavoidable and deliberate, so that partly formed opinions and new input from the day's key speakers could be built into the new context of sector groups.

Groups I, II and V

(comprising local authorities, schools, colleges of education, and curriculum development) discussed the following questions, and came to these conclusions.

Question 1

To what extent should or will the content of the school curriculum be affected by the new technologies?

(a) There was a strong urge to distinguish between information technology and the broad sweep of the new technologies. IT was seen as only a limited part of that broad development, but it achieved certain ends:

   (i) it made masses of information accessible which were previously unobtainable by the ordinary learner.

(ii) It produced direct evidence from the field, e.g. in video documentary material.
(iii) It could make information available in a form easier to assimilate than previous printed information.

(b) Evidence of changes in the content of subject teaching as a result of technological change were readily identified, for example:
(i) In modern languages, where the coming of language laboratories had quite radically altered syllabus content and changed the focus and balance of the subject.
(ii) In technical drawing, where computer-assisted design had changed the subject.
(iii) Typing and secretarial skills had been radically revised owing to changes in office technology.
(iv) Subjects like geography and modern studies had altered their approaches radically, introducing new topics and skills.
(v) In general, there was a shift away from lower order recall cognitive objectives to a more synthesised approach often founded on simulations and games, aimed at widening pupils' horizons, and introducing them to decision-making and the world of business.

(c) There was, in addition, the need to regard the study of the new technologies as a subject area in its own right, about which all pupils needed to have some awareness, though only a few might study the subject in depth. Fears of potential elitism coming from this were expressed but played down.
The recent statement by the Microelectronics, Computing and the Curriculum Project (MCC) of the CCC was favourably noted, although 'computer awareness across the curriculum' was preferred by some at S1 or S2. At earlier (primary school) stages, awareness would come from using the machines naturally as tools. The speed of change was such however that 'awareness' needed to be update, perhaps at S3 or S4 for pupils who had already had such a course in S1 or S2.

More detailed in-depth study to meet the needs of some pupils in secondary schools would be provided by the proposed O grade course in computer studies.

(d) Caution was expressed about a possible over-emphasis on the effects of the new technologies on the world of work and hence a possible neglect by schools of the need to retain for all pupils a strong thread of 'education for leisure', in no way inferior in status or approach to 'education for work', although 'We must not educate for unemployment, as many hitherto unsuspected job opportunities will emerge.

Question 2

What are the traditional processes of teaching/learning available to the teacher/learner? To what extent should these processes be *preserved* and to what extent *modified* by the new technologies?

Question 3

How can the new technologies be used to enrich the processes of teaching/learning?

The groups tended to take these two questions together.

(a) there was some objection to the use of the term 'processes' of teaching/learning as being too 'inhuman', and a tendency to focus on human relationships on human mediation or interaction, as the essential features of 'traditional processes' about the nature of which there was very little other agreement.

(b) A move away from class teaching to more group and individualised approaches was likely to be strengthened by the use of new equipment. The new technologies could give the means of learning directly to the pupil, thereby freeing time for the teacher to diagnose the weaknesses and problems of individual pupils. Suitable programmes would then assist in the provision of extension work for the more able and remedial work for the less so.

(c) This whole process would be assisted with the bigger classes in S1 and S2 by the adoption of more blocking in timetables and more extended units of time. The teacher's role would be to answer questions, promote discussion, motivate, deal with problems and generally work to realise the full potential of the new technology.

(d) An enrichment of the learning process could come from the wider range of stimuli from the new technologies, participation in decision-making exercises. Instant monitoring and feedback on progress, diagnostic assessment and remedial practice.

Question 4

What are the implications of our answers to these questions for (a) administrators? (b) curriculum planners? (c) teacher-trainers? (d) teachers?

(a) *Administrators.* The main priorities were seen as funding, the allocation of resources to staff development, and the purchase of adequate hardware and software. Local authorities mentioned the difficulty of having to allocate equally to all schools in their areas. The duty to ensure the release of staff to form working groups for preparing software and undertaking module and course construction was also stressed. The special role of the Scottish Education Department in funding and curriculum development was underlined.

(b) *Curiculum planners.* Groups stressed the need to involve industrialists and avoid over-lengthy consuitatations in what should be an on-going and responsive process. Well planned modular structures for courses would allow for quicker response to demand.

(c) *Teacher-trainers and teachers.* The need for retraining led groups to consider these two together. The training system was alleged to find it dificult to strike a balance between giving student-teachers 'survival skills' for the classroom, and encouraging them to look into the future and to assess the need for change. Updating of training staff was also a necessity. One group insisted that all intending teachers needed to have some industrial experience and to be trained in the use of microcomputers.

(d) One group felt that *politicians* should have been listed as a category in this question. The political will to make the resources available for the new developments would be crucial.

Groups III and IV

(comprising industry, further education, and higher education other than colleges of education) discussed the following questions and came to these conclusions.

Question 1

What are the central aims that must be preserved in education and training programmes in any new situations, taking fully into account the needs of the *learners, society,* and the *systems* in which the learners operate?

(a) There was the same tendency as on the day before to assert that general aims would remain fairly constant. Training aims could alter with every situation, but in general they did not. On the other hand, objectives altered according to societal needs and individual potentials. The role of the new technologies as the main agents of change was again questioned.

(b) There was some reluctance to focus on the needs of society, although it was alleged that further education colleges were more aware of these than schools. They attempted, for example, to redefine patterns of work and leisure, and to shift the balance of education and training from the manufacturing to the service sector.

(c) The needs of individuals and of the systems were seen as closely linked. While objectives relating to standards and practical skills had to be established, these could include aspects of personal development. Any conflict between the needs of the systems (especially industry) and those of the individual was likely to affect discipline and motivation adversely.

(d) It was argued that educational aims related broadly to a preparation for life, and learning was to be seen as a life-long process. Predicting change was difficult, and better based on a dialogue between teachers and learners than on a teacher's or counsellor's vision of the future.

Question 2

How will the government 'Action Plan' for 16 -18s in Scotland affect the *patterns and processes* of training, and how can or will these be *assisted* by innovations in information technology?

(a) The Action Plan received a cautious welcome although there was insufficient real knowledge about its intentions. It was felt to apply primarily to training and to be particularly relevant to further education institution rather than to secondary schools. This was a matter of concern to some members.

(b) It was hoped that the 'flexibility' mentioned in the Action Plan would apply to learning methods and processes as well as to content. With reference to the modular structures of courses, therefore, it was argued that the teacher would have to analyse the module and then *together with the learners* develop a learning programme suited to local needs.

(c) Information technology could assist in developing the individualised and negotiated approach to curriculum which would be necessary, and in providing the necessary information base for the counselling and guidance service that would now become essential.

Question 3

Do adult learners require a different provision?

(a) Some anxiety was expressed about the 'naivety' of the question, unless it was to be interpreted to mean 'How different should adult provision be from that made for 16 -18s? Other members felt the need to establish that there must be some provision for adults in the first place, before discussing how different it should be.

(b) Differences were felt to lie in the greater capacity of adults to take control of their own learning situations. They were frequently highly motivated and accustomed to working on their own with minimal external organisation of their work. Flexibility of learning time and learning patterns was stressed, and open learning development were felt to suit adults' varied patterns of life and work best.

(c) Practical reservations were expressed about the lack of suitable learning materials. Adults could cope better with independent or resource-based learning, but there was doubt about the possibilities of extending open learning methods unless there was a major input of resources into materials development.

Question 4

What implications do our answers to these questions have for (a) training programmes? (b) the training of trainers? (c) institutions or firms of different sizes?

(a) *Training programmes.* The need was expressed to disseminate and exchange software once the training programmes had been developed in high technology terms. This was essential, to achieve economy of scale and to avoid duplication of effort. The efforts of the Scottish Microelectronics Development Programme were noted in this respect. So also was the work of the Council for Educational Technology to develop downline facilities via Prestel to facilitate the spread of established and vetted training programmes. Large authorities could develop their own viewdata systems and download programmes to both formal educational institutions and commercial or industrial users.

(b) *The training of trainers.* This aspect dominated group discussion, there being almost equal agreement on the need for major staff development programmes and on the almost insurmountable problems of finding time for staff to participate. Inflexible requirements for attendance patterns on courses were criticised. More flexible strategies were felt to be possible, through open learning approaches and the employment of self-assessment techniques for the learners. Industrial training staff were held to better at handling these problems, and the lack of liaison between educational and industrial trainers was criticised.

(c) *Institutions or firms of different sizes.* It was argued that resource-based or independent learning/training programmes developed by large firms or institutions could probably be used in most locations regardless of size, mainly because of new developments in information technology. The preponderance of small firms in the Scottish context was also noted.

Conference Organiser's Final Comment

Inevitably all groups felt the pressure of time, and the closing stages of discussions were always hurried. The central themes of the conference, that trainers in education and industry face the same types of problems from the coming of the new technologies and that these same technologies would be the sources of the solutions, seemed to be borne out in the discussions. There were many comments on how enlightening and stimulating these had been, and on the need to pursue the debates further in some other common forum, either in SCET or elsewhere. Initiatives by the CCC, individual colleges of education or further education and others all point along the same line.

3

Workshops and Seminars for Technical Education

Introduction

Part of the conference programme consisted of a menu of workshops and seminars. Because of their varied nature, not all of these sessions lend themselves to written reports. Several were largely practical, while others took the form of lively dialogue. Still others are to a large extent covered by existing publications, and where this is the case the reader is directed to the list of references at the end of this chapter.

Three of the workshop sessions are, however, reported here at some length. Even so, unfortunately, each paper can give only the barest bones of what actually took place during the session. In the case of the interactive video workshop, only one of the possible papers is included because, in such a rapidly developing field, it was felt best to concentrate on those technical aspects likely to have the most permanent relevance. The paper on MAIL which is included describes the system, but, of course, the full benefit of the workshop came from the interaction of the participants with the machine and the presenter. Finally, in his presentation on open learning, Nigel Paine took participants through an existing Prestel programme and extended this with pages specially set up on the SCET viewdata system. These pages are presented here, but sadly without the colour that gives them added impact.

The full list of workshops is given below, followed by papers on Interactive Video by John Duke, on MAIL by Richard Freeman, and on Open Learning by Nigel Paine.

List of Workshops

Viewdata in Business

Presenter: John Martin

This on-line demonstration covered the different business uses of Prestel and private viewdata systems. No prior knowledge of viewdata was assumed, and the demonstration moved on from basic ideas to cover the existing facilities of viewdata: communication of up-to-date information; electronic mail, Prestel gateway to third party computers. Future development of viewdata systems was also considered.

Viewdata in Education

Presenter: Dennis W. Daly

The different uses of Prestel and private viewdata system in education were covered in this on-line demonstration. The demonstration started with basic ideas and considered the following viewdata applications: information about education; quizzes, games and tests; learning materials; electronic mail and telesoftware. Future developments of viewdata systems were also considered.

Telesoftware

Presenters: Dennis W. Daly and John Martin

Viewdata systems can be used to store and transmit computer programmes (rather than pages of text) to modified microeconomics and this important capability gives viewdata systems the potential to provide an electronic software distribution network which can transmit programmes from a central point to the growing number of microcomputers in schools, homes and offices. A demonstration of telesoftware was given and the seminar considered the feasibility and costs of establishing and using such an electronic software distribution network.

Information Technology and Open Learning: Analogues of Interactivity

Presenter: Nigel Paine

The presentation showed that the progress made over the last five years in the design of interactive printed material needs to find specific analogues in other media, if we are not simply to repeat the same mistakes made with print in the early stages of learning materials design.

Interactive Video

Presenters: John Duke, The Council for Educational Technology Diana. M Laurillard, Institute of Educational Technology, The Open University

Alistair Stewart, Dundee College of Technology

John Duke was carrying out a survey for CET on interactive video and its implications for education and training. He introduced the topic and gave an up-to-the-minute picture of what was happening worldwide.

In the first phase of a pilot study of interactive video, Diana Laurillard was experimenting with a programme designed to introduce the concepts involved in signals in communication. She described the study and discussed the educational implications of the new medium as well as the logistic and administrative problems it presents.

Dundee College of Technology has been investigating the interaction between microcomputers and a variety of audio-visual media. Alistair Stewart described some of their developments with particular emphasis on the video-disc.

Video in Training

Presenter: Robert W. Rowatt

This illustrated lecture explored the various ways in which video can be used to assist learning in the context of industrial training. Particular reference was made to single camera portable systems and examples were shown of the medium in use in different modes.

'Making the Most of What Little You've Got'

Presenter: Robert W. Rowatt

This was a demonstration lecture intended to show how various media and their associated equipment can assist in video production, particularly with single camera portable equipment.

The emphasis was on obtaining effective results as cheaply as possible.

Broadcasting and the New Technologies: The New Technologies

Presenter: Joe F. Murray

Brief presentations by contributors from broadcasting and education were made in the course of this seminar.

An examination was made of the educational potential of new forms of audito-visual technology: what opportunities do things like cable television and satellite broadcasting offer to schools, colleges and local authorities? What effect will their adoption have on the educational provision currently made by the broadcasting companies?

Broadcasting and the New Technologies: Implication for Education

Presenter: Joe F. Murray

Brief presentations by contributors form broadcasting and education were made in the course of this seminar.

An informative description was given of the technological changes that are likely to affect audio-visual communication (cable, satellites, etc.) and of the effects that the adoption of such technologies might have on the structure of broadcasting.

MAIL: Micro Aided Learning

Presenter: Richard Freeman

A demonstration by the National Extension College of the microcomputer system which they use to provide response to student assignments designed to support the Channel 4 Numeracy Series. As students complete their assignments these are posted to the National Extension College, who are able to provide through MAIL a rapid computerised response to the student's work on the assignment, personally addressed to each student. The system works with the BBC microcomputer and disc drive. The National Extension College intends to license the system to other users.

OPTICAL DISC TECHNOLOGY AND INTERACTIVE VIDEO

Disc Technology

The video-disc has recently become commercially available in Europe. Philips launched LaserVision on the domestic market during the summer of 1982, primarily as a consumer entertainment product. This was a simple player unit for direct connection to a standard television set, and it came with a catalogue of a few dozen video programmes, mostly transfers from film and video-tape. Video-disc has indeed been available in the United States for some years and in the NTSC format there are currently three competing systems. Selectavision, developed by the Radio Corporation of America, uses a grooved disc with diamond stylus riding in the groove and retrieving the signal by detecting changes in capacitance. A second Capacitance Electronic Disc (CED) system has been developed by the Japanese JVC Company. This design, known as Video High Density (VHD), involves a flat stylus gliding over the surface of a smooth disc and detecting changes in capacitance of a video signal encoded as a series of pits laid down on a spiral track within the disc. The third system is LaserVision, which employs optical recording and laser technology. They are all incompatible.

A number of other vidio-disc systems have reached prototype stage, and some have been subject to limited marketing exercises. Among these may be mentioned the early Decca-Telefunken TelDec mechanical system; the ARDEV photographic system now owned by McDonnell Douglas; and the Thomson-CSF laser-based system that has certain similarities to LaserVision. Although the Thorn-EMI company has made preparations to introduce the VHD capacitance system into Europe, the only system that is currently available on the PAL television standard in LaserVision. For this reason, and since the system has many features of interest to education and training, this report will tend to concentrate on LaserVision.

Video-disc technology is aimed at providing an inexpensive way of storing television programmes and to succeed has to demonstrate effectively advantages over magnetic tape recording systems. The disc offers compact, relatively low cost storage. It is portable, rugged and environmentally stable. The LaserVision disc carries a protective coating which makes it virtually immune to scratches and surface contamination. It can be readily replicated from a master stamping. Whereas it cannot be locally re-recorded, as can magnetic tape, it is, unlike the video-cassette, a truly random access device which allows any individual video image to be rapidly retrieved. Further, it can tolerate endless repetition of a single image in still-frame mode, and sequences can be played with clarity and precision at any speed up to three times normal television rate in both forwards and reverse directions. These properties, and the fact that playback equipment can be designed so that all functions can be controlled by an external computer, have aroused significant interest in the context of education and training.

The LaserVision optical video-disc carries in a single information channel a composite signal containing all that is necessary to reproduce a high quality colour television picture, together with two accompanying sound tracks and associated control data. The original television signal is used to pulsate a finely focused laser beam in the master recording equipment, producing a series of pits on the surface of a glass disc coated with a light sensitive layer. A nickel stamper copy is produced from the master and this is used to replicate plastic copies. Each plastic replica is coated with an aluminium layer to make it more reflective, and a thin protective coat of clear plastic added. Copy discs are read back in a player unit fitted with a low-power helium-neon laser which is focused through the protective layer on to the aluminised relief. The reflected beam is converted by a photodiode into an electrical signal that is demodulated and processed to regenerate an exact copy of the original video signal ready for display on a normal television receiver.

The standard LaserVision disc is 30 centimeters in diameter. Information is recorded in a continuous spiral from the centre of the disc to the outside, revolving anti-clockwise as viewed by the laser beam. Due to the very small size of the pits the disc can contain 55,000 tracks, each of which can be separately resolve. By arranging for the speed of revolution of the disc (1500 rpm) to correspond exactly to the framing rate of the television signal, each 'track' corresponds to a single frame (two fields). This arrangement makes it possible to achieve still frame and slow motion replay by reading the same track more than once, the optical beam jumping back during the vertical synchronisation interval.

Other information is also recorded on the disc. Each frame is given an absolute picture number to identify it, and it is also possible to insert chapter numbers to indicate the beginning of a new sequence. Such data is digitally coded on lines within the vertical blanking interval, which do not normally carry picture information. These lines may also carry stop codes and other control information by which the player can be programmed to execute certain functions. If played continuously, a single video-disc side offers about 37 minutes' playing time. The major interest in education, however, is obviously in programmed, intermittent action, when incorporated in an interactive video system.

Playback Equipment

Playback equipment may be characterised by the range of facilities provided. Simple domestic video-disc players such as the Philips VP 700 are self-contained units operated by means of a push-button keyboard control. These have individual frame addressability and include still frame, slow, fast and reverse motion, but have no extensive programming power. They are not suitable for interactive operations. The Pioneer LP1100 domestic video-disc player, however, is interesting since it is possible to simulate the action of its remote control keyboard from an external microcomputer, and thus employ the player as a component of an interactive, programmable system. An interface to connect the Pioneer player to a BBC microcomputer has been developed by Michael Grove and marketed by Acorn Computers Ltd.

Philips has produced a limited number of Professional LaserVision VP705 Players. This again has a remote control handset to control all the player functions, and in addition has certain memory facilities so that a sequence of operations can be pre-programmed. More importantly, the player is provided with a two-way serial communications interface to RS-232-C standard. Via this connector an external computer can send instructions to the player, and receive information back in return. This allows an external computer to take complete control of all the player functions, and display in any order any frame or sequence on the disc. Additionally, the computer may be programmed to interpose comment, questions, or other material, from its own memory which can be displayed on the same screen as the video images. To facilitate this, the VP705 is fitted with a teletext encoder by means of which teletext characters and graphics may be generated.

With a suitably equipped external computer, such a system could be connected with a remote viewdata data-base. In this manner permanent information, high quality pictures and sound would be stored on the video-disc, while volatile information was provided via the viewdata link.

Compiling an Interactive Programme

Facilities are thus available for teachers and trainers to begin to experiment with the use of video-disc as an instructional medium. There are a number of hurdles to be overcome, however, in the compilation of an interactive video-disc programme. To make a master video-disc requires a broadcast quality transcription vidio-tape to at least 1 inch type C standard, fully edited and complete with synchronised time-code. The programme may well contain a series of short segments, and may be many single images. This can entail a formidable editing task and requires professional facilities.

Video segments will normally be produced by standard studio methods, but may also be culled from existing footage. It is clear, however, that to take greatest advantage of the new medium a different design philosophy needs to be adopted from that which has evolved in conventional educational television. For instance, programme elements may not be viewed continuously, or necessarily consecutively; certain elements will be used and re-used by the same viewer and should be free of irritating features; certain elements will require to be regularly updated; and it is not necessary, or even desirable, to regard the video medium as the sole carrier of the massage.

The capacity of the video-disc to support random access to large numbers of still images makes it a powerful medium for storing visual data-bases. It is necessary to remember, however, the different aspect ratio of the television screen to that of the photographic slide, and that the relatively poor resolution of television will cause fine detail to blur or disappear altogether. Pages of text may be stored on video-disc by considering them as equivalent to still images, but there are limitations to the type and quantity of print that can be accommodated on a normal television screen. The optimum capacity is no more than 30 lines of 64 characters each, and a conventional A4 document would require eight television pages to offer satisfactory reproduction.

Text may conveniently be created in teletext formal and stored on floppy discs or other memory associated with a linked computer system. Text, questions and response inviting routines stored in this way and other aspects of computer programming have to be considered alongside the production of the visual sequences. A comprehensive flow chart of the evolving programme becomes a vital production aid, particularly if a number of branching features and re-entrant loops are incorporated.

To assist production planning, and to help in the generation of textual and response frames, a range of authoring languages and systems is available that may be adapted to video-disc production. These systems also provide for analysis of student responses in order to determine consequent action. All the techniques of computer-aided learning may be employed - tutorial mode, drill and practice, simulation, and so on - dependent on the power of the associated microcomputer and the specific objective of the programme. One interesting concept is that of an unprogrammed compilation of materials on video-disc - a resource disc - that may be used with a simple programming scheme by a local teacher to produce individually directed course elements. The system devised by Acorn Computers incorporates the Microtext authoring language in an ROM chip that can be used in this manner and offers a low cost entry into interactive video.

It is inevitable in the early stages of development that emphasis is placed on the technical issues. However, successful acceptance of interactive video systems will be largely influenced by the range and quality of teaching programmes that can be made available. The design and production of interactive video demands the integration of many professional skills in a team enterprise, including:

- subject expertise and authoring
- teaching and curriculum development
- instructional design and evaluation
- text editing and graphic design
- computer proramming and system engineering
- film and television production
- project direction and budgetary management.

The Future for Interactive Video

A number of the issues that have to be faced by organisations wishing to participate in the development of interactive video for education and training are discussed in a recent working paper published by the Council for Educational Technology. The report suggests that a co-operative development programme should be initiated to produce a significant quantity of material for evaluation. If is can be shown the interactive video can play a vital part in many educational and training situations, and there is a strong possibility that this is in fact so, then the technique could become the basis of a new 'knowledge-based' industry. For these reasons, it is suggested that industrial participation should be sought at the outset from the electronics and computer industries, from publishers and media distributors, and from the television and telecommunication fields.

Interactive video exemplifies the powerful possibilities that result from the convergence of the new information and communication technologies. Combining television and CAL techniques promises a basis for an important new educational and training tool with unique characteristics. It may be predicted that interactive video will become a significant component of a future 'electronic learning station', capable of bringing to the individual learner a rich variety of resources and facilities, and adaptable to a wide spectrum of educational tasks.

References

Laurillard, D. (1982), 'The Potential of Interactive Video'. *Journal of Educational Television* 8, III.

Rowatt, R. W. (1980), *Video*, SCET, Glasgow, Scotland.

Murray, J. F. (1982), *The Future of Educational Broadcasting*. SCET, Glasgow Scotland.

CET (1983), *Interactive Video: Implications for Education and Training*. Working Paper No. 22, CET, London, England.

4

Micro Aided Learning

Origins

All distance teaching institutions grapple with a recurring problem: how to reduce drop-out rates. Many factors are thought to influence drop-out and much research has been carried out in order to try and identify these. Recently, research in Norway has indicated that assignment turn-round time is the single most important factor influencing student progress. If a student receives his assignment back within six days of posting it, the return of the assignment seems to motivate the student to continue with his course. Longer turn-round times seem to result in a low motivation to continue studying. It is clear therefore that distance teaching institutions have to find ways of reducing turn-round times, if possible to below six days. This is not, in fact, practicable. Assignments have to make three postal journeys and tutors have to find time to mark them. But if human tutors cannot achieve a fast enough turn-round time, can computers do it instead?

Relationships to Earlier Systems

What was required was not in fact new. At least two systems had already been developed to do a similar job. These were CADE (in Sweden) and RSVP (in the USA). Both were investigated as possible solutions but both suffered from two major disadvantages. First, they used large main-frame computers and second, they required a high level of technical skill to set up and run. These systems seemed to lack the cheapness and flexibility of modern microcomputer based systems. True, perhaps, developing an easy to use microcomputer based system might reduce the number of features which the system could offer, but the result could be a faster, better to use, ultra-cheap system. The design of MAIL was therefore a compromise.

MAIL in Outline

MAIL is best described by starting with a brief outline of what it offers the student MAIL was designed for home-based students studying under the tutorial guidance of a remote distance learning centre. At the end of a block of study (say, one week's work), the student finds a MAIL test in his course. This consists of up to 10 questions, each with up to four answers to choose from. The student selects what he considers to be the correct answer to each question and enters A, B, C or D in the appropriate box on his MAIL Answerr Form (Figure 4.1). He posts the form to the distance teaching centre. Using first class post within England, over 90 per cent of forms will arrive at the centre by 8 a.m. on the following day.

National Extension College Mail answer from

MAIL : Micro Aided Learning

Please complete one MAIL answer form for each MAIL test that you do.

Title Mr/Mrs/Miss/Ms

Initials: □□□□□□

Name : □□□□□□□□□□□□□

Address : □□□□□□□□□□□□□

Town : □□□□□□□□□□□□□

Postcode: □□□□□□□□□□

Enter your MAIL student number

CM □□□□□□

Enter the details for this MAIL test :

Course name : ____________

Course Number : ____________

Test Number □

Enter your answers (A, B, C or D) for each question in the test:

Question	1	2	3	4	5	6	7	8	9	10
Answer										

When you have completed this test post it to MAIL TESTS, NATIONAL EXTENSION COLLEGE, 18 BROOKLANDS AVENUE, CAMBRIDGE CB22HN.

Please enclose a stamped addressed envelope for your MAIL reply.

Fig. 4.1: MAIL answer form.

An operator then enters the student's number, course number, test number and answers into the microcomputer. Up to 50 forms can be entered in one run. The computer marks each test and prints out a detailed personal letter, selecting comments from a comment file according to the responses the student has given. A typical letter will be two pages long.

As each test in marked, the student's personal file is updated to record his mark and the date on which the test was marked. By 12 p.m., his MAIL letter is in the post and should reach him by 8 a.m. on the following day - a turn-round time of 36 - 48 hours.

The Structure of MAIL

MAIL consists currently of six computer progammes which are accessed from the menu shown in Figure 4.2.

TEST MARKING PROGRAMME

1 Mark tests
2 Amend a course file
3 Amend student file
4 Create new student file
5 Create new course file
6 Enrol Students
7 Print course file proof
8 Print statistics
9 End

Key No. required:

Fig. 4.2: The MAIL menu.

The system requires a BBC microcomputer attached to a double disc drive and printer. For each course, menu option 2 is used to place a comments file on side 2 of a disc. (The programme suite is placed on side 1 of the comments disc.) Menu 4 is used to create a student file of up to 1000 students on a second disc. Once that has been done the programme suite is used for three major tasks:

- entering comments on the comment file
- enrolling students
- marking tests.

These will be considered in turn.

The Comment File

Everything that goes into this file is determined by the lecturer in charge of the course. For each course for which he wishes to create a comment file, he specifies the following:

- number of tests in the course (maximum 15).

Then for each test he specifies:

- number of questions (maximum 10)
- number of sub-groups into which questions will be split (1- 3)
- correct option for each response on each question (A, B, C or D)
- mark for each option (0 - 10)
- questions to be allocated to each sub-group
- comment for each option (maximum 510 characters)
- comment for performance on each sub-block (maximum 255 characters)
- introductory paragraph (maximum 510 characters)
- closing paragraph (maximum 510 characters.)

Menu option 2 is designed to allow this material to be entered on to the file (or amended) by a typist. No more than one hour's training is needed for this task, since no knowledge of computing is necessary. After the comments are entered, the operator prints out a proof copy with menu option 7 which is sent to the lecturer for proof reading.

The Student File

Students are enrolled with menu option 6. For each student, the operator enters the student's name, address and course number. The programme allocates a student number with a modulo 11 check digit and optionally, allows the entering of another student number (e.g. college reference number) and tutor number. Most other access to this file is by the marking programme which uses the student file to retrieve names and addresses and to record marks.

What has MAIL Achieved?

Mail has the following valuable features:

(a) It uses cheap, readily available microcomputing equipment (microcomputer £532; disc drive £700; printer £400; monitor £120).

(b) Lecturers can use it with no knowledge of computers. All that they have to do is to fill in a booklet specifying what they want on their comment file.

(c) All keyboard operations can be carried out by a typist. The total system can be mastered in a few hours.

(d) Although cheap, any one student disc can cater for up to 1000 students. (A mark 2 version will cater for 2000 students.) If that is insufficient capacity, further student discs an be created.

(e) Letters can be turned round at very high speed. A two-page letter takes tow minutes to generate, so one MAIL system can handle in excess of 50,000 tests per year.

Limitations

MAIL has two limitations: one derived from the software, one from the hardware.

One the software side, MAIL does not offer complex commenting of the type 'If the student did less well on this test than the last test and he has missed three classes . . .' It was felt that such systems are too complex for lecturers to use, requiring days of work to produce comments for just one test. MAIL is easy for lecturers to use and so has the prospect of being used.

The hardware limitation arises from using diskettes rather than hard discs. With diskettes, all tests on one run must be on one course - the course whose comment disc is currently in the drive. If the system were to be adapted to hard disc (not currently available on the BBC microcomputer), then dozens of comment files could be on line, alongwith 5000 - 10,000 students.

INFORMATION TECHNOLOGY AND OPEN LEARNING

Aims of the Session

1. To examine the context of non-print based learning material.
2. To outline analogues of the interactive qualities of print based learning material.
3. To demonstrate the application of those analogues to a particular training course on Prestel.

What is Open Learning?

Any open learning system will have three separate but interrelated elements, which can be shown diagrammatically as follows:

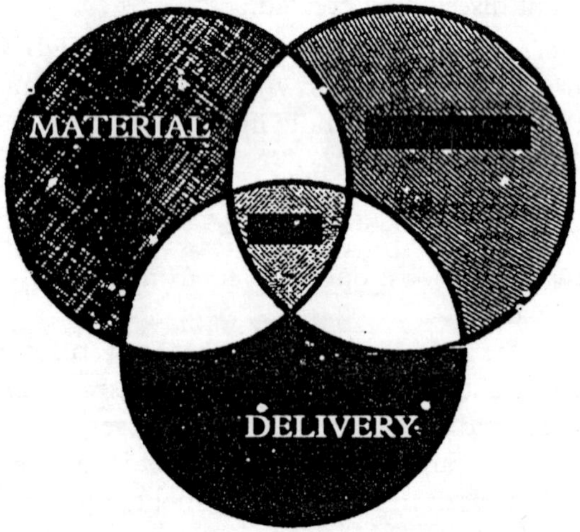

The elements are the learning resources themselves, which can consist of only one medium, or of multi-media resources, the delivery system for those resources, and the support system used to help the trainee or student learn from them.

The open learning system lies at the intersection of those three elements. The nature of the resources may well dictate the sort of delivery system or the support needed; the kind of support which can be offered will affect the learning resources and therefore the delivery system. An open learning system is not, therefore, any pre-structured formula, but a system designed around the needs of the learner, taking account of available facilities, existing constraints and appropriate resources. This can be expressed in the form of a diagram, as below:

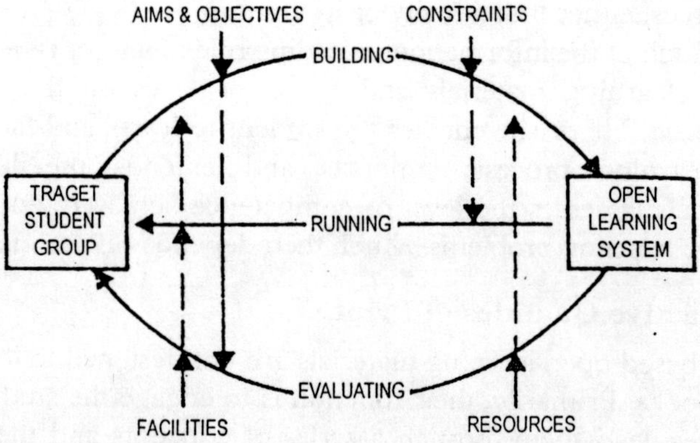

An open learning system can be operated just as will within a single company location as it can across grat distances, far from the learning centre which is running the course.

If we list the following polarities:

Flexible attendance	Fixed attendance
Open access	Restricted access
Open entry	Fixed entry points
Open ended	Fixed finishing point
Learner negotiated curriculum	Curriculum fixed by centre or examination body

the open learning system will tend to have most of these characteristics to the left of the dotted line. It would be very dificult to imagine an open learning system with a very fixed attendance pattern; limited access at only one time of the year; or a curriculum which was non-negotiable and had to be completed by a particular date.

Lack of flexibility in one or two areas does not, however, preclude the development of an open learning system. In fact, because the course is learner centred, it has to be tailored to a particular target group, and this tends to deny access to others.

The Primacy of Learning Resources

The key feature of an open learning system is the separation of teacher and learner. They may be in the same building, but the essential pattern of an open learning system is learning through resources, either individually or in a group.

Much of the information providing role of a tutor is devolved to the learning materials and the tutor takes on the role of *animateur.* He or she enables the student to learn, and facilitates the learning process; supports and extends the learning materials; assesses the level of competence achieved; and helps resolve learning problems. Much then depends on the materials.

Interactive Qualities of Print

Print based open learning materials are not designed to look like text books. Primarily, their function is to engage the students or trainees, lead them through a series of concepts and then help them test their grasp of them.

Rather than aiming for passive consumption of the text, the material attempts to encourage the students to participate actively in learning. In order to do this, certain key features need to be embodied in any print based material.

Roger Lewis defines the characteristics of self-study materials:

- making clear to the learner what he needs to know or be able to do
- providing objectives
- giving the learner the chance to see how well he is monitoring the objectives by provideing self-assessment questions and answers in the text
- giving any necessary study advice
- unpacking difficult concepts
- breaking up the subject into manageable chunks for study
- conversing with the student or trainee in lively, friendly and informal way.

I would add to this list:

- signposting the material carefully and continually
- offering some form of 'help' sequence if the learner encounters problems
- reviewing what has been dealt with at regular intervals
- allowing the opportunity for systematic evaluation of the materials by the learner.

These characteristic make print material interactive, yet many attempts to move from print into any other medium ignore them. Some expensive electronic data-bases offer no more than a page turning sequence for the learner, based on poor programmed learning techniques.

Analogues for Other Media

Of the characteristics stated, several should have an analogue in any other medium used, if the resources are to be used successfully in an open learning system.

It is up to the instructional designer to find the specific analogue for the print characteristic, and the analogue will vary depending on the nature of the delivery system. However, a package in any medium should possess:

- a list of learning outcomes or objectives
- an indication of the nature and scope of the package
- self-assessment in a variety of forms, exploiting the nature of the medium to the full
- a user-friendly tone and relationship between the component parts of the system
- a well structured and clearly signposted data-base
- frequent review/revision sequences
- provision for student evaluation of the material
- a help sequence in case of difficulty.

No particular medium is intrinsically better for the delivery of self-learning material; effectiveness will depend on the number of characteristics from print built in as analogues.

We can re-package the list into:

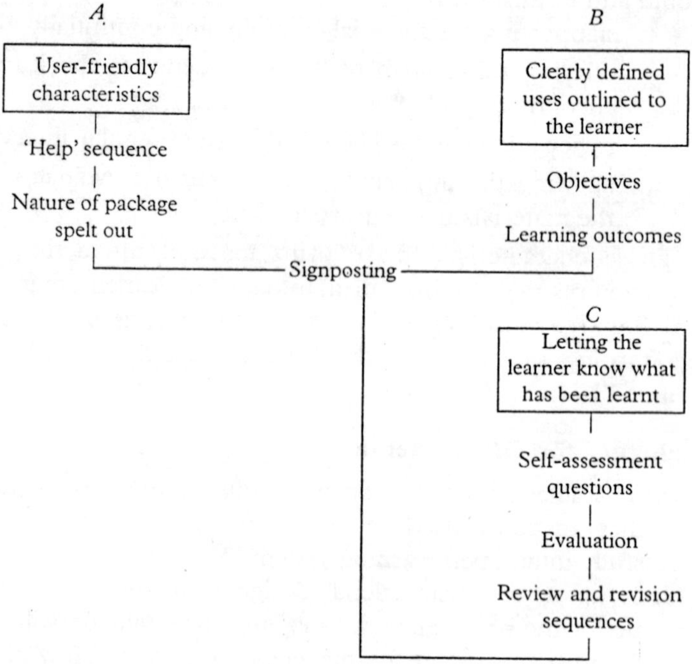

A Worked Example

To see how this can work, we looked at a very good case study designed to update doctors and located within the BMJ/Glaxo data-base on Prestel. This data-base (closed to all except doctors) offers a wide variety of information packages, including current appointments and summaries of *British Medical Journal* leading articles. The title page is reproduced below:

Within the Glaxo index (key 9) is a series of options, including seven Prestel case studies:

BMJ/GLAXO 2650a Op
BRITISH MEDICAL JOURNAL – GLAXO
1. APPOINTMENTS
2. PARTNERSHIPS – OFFERED/WANTED
3. BMJ CONTENTS – 27 AUGUST
4. BMA BOOKLIST
5. YOUR OPINION WOULD BE WELCOME
9. GLAXO INDEX
Last Updated – Friday 26 August

BMJ/GLAXO 26591a Op

BMJ/GLAXO SERVICE TO DOCTORS

DIFFERENTIAL DIAGNOSIS NO. 1

High Fever in a Child
A programme for doctors
based on an actual case

CLINCIAL CONSULTANT
P.E. Gower Consultant Physican
Charise Cross Hospital London
EDUCATIONAL ADVISER
R.MCG Larger Proffesor of Medical
Education, Durcbce University

WHEN READY TO START KEY 1

BMJ/GLAXO 265910a Op

IT IS 9 O'CLOCK ON A SUNDAY MORNING

Dr. Andrews receives a telephone call from Mrs. Baker.

Her daughter Anne, aged 5, has been running a high temperature for the past two days.

The Child has vomited once but there has been no diarrhoea.

Dr. Andrews tells the mother that he will call to see Anne.

KEY 1 TO CONTINUE

BMJ/GLAXO 2659101a Op

HE CALLS AT THE HOUSE

Mrs. Baker tells him that Anne has had one or two similar but less severe attacks in the past year. She has treated these successfully.

Sometimes the urine has been strong, cloudy and smelly with occasionally pain on passing water.

KEY 1 TO CONTINUE

BMJ/GLAXO 2659102a Op

On examination, Dr. Andrews finds that the child has a temperature of 40'C and a pluse rate of 140 per min.

There is rebound tenderness in the right side of the abdomen and tenderness in the right loin. Bowel sounds are reduced but present :

The hernial orifices are normal. No evidence is apparent of a rash or Iynahadenopathy.

The mouth, throat and ears appear normal.

There are no abnormal signs in the chest.

Neck stiffiness and jaundice are absent.

KEY 1 TO CONTINUE

BMJ/GLAXO 2659103a Op

WHAT IS THE LIKELY CLINICAL DIAGNOSIS?

1. Urinary Tract Intrection
2. Appemnicitis
3. Measeteric Adenities
4. Virus Infection
5. Other febrite condition of childhood e.g. middle ear infection pheumonia.
6. An Exanthema

KEY NUMBER ACCORDING TO YOUR CHOICE

BMJ/GLAXO 26591036a Op

NO. THERE IS NO EVIDENCE ON EXAMINATION OF AN EXANTHEMA

KEY 0 AND MAKE ANOTHER CHOICE

FOR FURTHER INFORMATION ABOUT EXANTHEMA - KEY 8

- High fever in a child
- Patient with a common gastrointestinal disorder
- An unusual complication of pregnancy
- Recurrent 'bronchitis'?
- The Dyspeptic's Tale
- Failure to thrive
- Eczema in a housewife.

We looked at the case study on high fever in a child. This takes doctors through a case history concerning an undiagnosed fever in a small child. It begins with three pages of information before asking the doctors to choose a likely clinical diagnosis given the information provided. The example overleaf shows an incorrect choice.

After the initial diagnosis, the child is admitted to hospital and various test results are fed into the case study to help the doctors make their choice of diagnosis.

There is no instant 'correct' solution; the programme is a differential diagnosis where various options are systematically eliminated as more information is known. Each false route chosen - such as the exanthema routing above - offers further information explaining why this was a poor choice at that particular moment. Once he has digested this information, the doctor is routed back into the mainline of the data-base until he reaches a final diagnosis (in this case, of reflex nephropathy caused by a proteus infection of the urinary tract). Learners are finally asked to evaluate the case study using response pages which are sent back immediately to the information providers.

I have drawn up a simple routing system for the first half of the case study. This is a branching system which needs a doctor's

BMJ/GLAXO 265819a Op

FINAL COMMENTS

UTI in children is often difficult to diagnose. In the content of this child's illness an appendicectony was unavoidable.

If an upper uranary tract intection is suspected this must be treated adequately with an effective antibioted for at least one weel.

In children parteriolosically ....
....

BMJ/GLAXO 265819a Op

FINAL COMMENTS Continued

A proteus intection of the urinary tract suggests renal rather than bladder involvement.

If severe reflux nephropathy is present surgery and careful follow up may be required. Minor degrees of reflux disappear with age.

Parents can be reassured that generally the outlook for children with reflux nephropathy is good.

THIS IS THE END OF THE FIRST PROGRAMME PLEASE KEY 1

interaction in order to make progress through the data-base. It is sell designed and well structured as learning material.

The programme is essentially linear, covering the early diagnosis, admission to hospital, further tests, the operation and so on. At each stage, small circular routes lead the doctor from the main track and back to the linear path. Information and updating are provided at each point of intersection.

BMJ/GLAXO 2658195a Op

DIFFERENTIAL DIAGNOSIS NO. 1
YOUR OPINION WOULD BE APPRECIATED

Names: Scot Council for Educ.Tech how Useful did you find the Programme key on the scale from 1 (of little use) to 5 (very useful).
How Appropriate to your Requirements was the level
Key from 1 (too easy)
to 5 (too difficult) __ (key)
Key : to send, Key not to send

BMJ/GLAXO 2659196a Op

DIFFERENTIAL DIAGNOSIS NO. 1
To help in the evaluation of the programme would you please key the appropriate number:
AREYOU:

1. Community Health Service Doctor
2. Consultant
3. General Practitioner trainnes?
4. General Practitioner trainee?
5. General Practitioner vocational trainer?
6. House officer?
7. Registrar
8. Senior Register
9. Other doctor

SCOT COUNCIL FOR EDUC.TECH

The routing map shows that there are four main intersections: two major ones which list many alternatives, each of which provides further information; and two minor ones requiring a yes or no answer with follow-up page if required.

This is a structure to which viewdata is ideally suited, given its branching system of indexing.

Modifications of the Data-base

I make now a series of suggestions for incorporating my own list of analogues into what is already sophisticated learning material, and an analysis of the effect of doing this. My suggestions are only examples, which I generated on the SCET private viewdata system and stored separately from the Prestel data-base. They have never been tested 'live' on doctors using the real BMJ/Glaxo data-base, but a simulation of the combined data-base was positively evaluated by a doctor prior to this workshop.

Additional Page 1

My first modification is an additional starter page (see below). Instead of plunging doctors straight into the case study, I have offered three choices. First they can begin the case study in the normal way. Or, if they are dubious about the value of the case

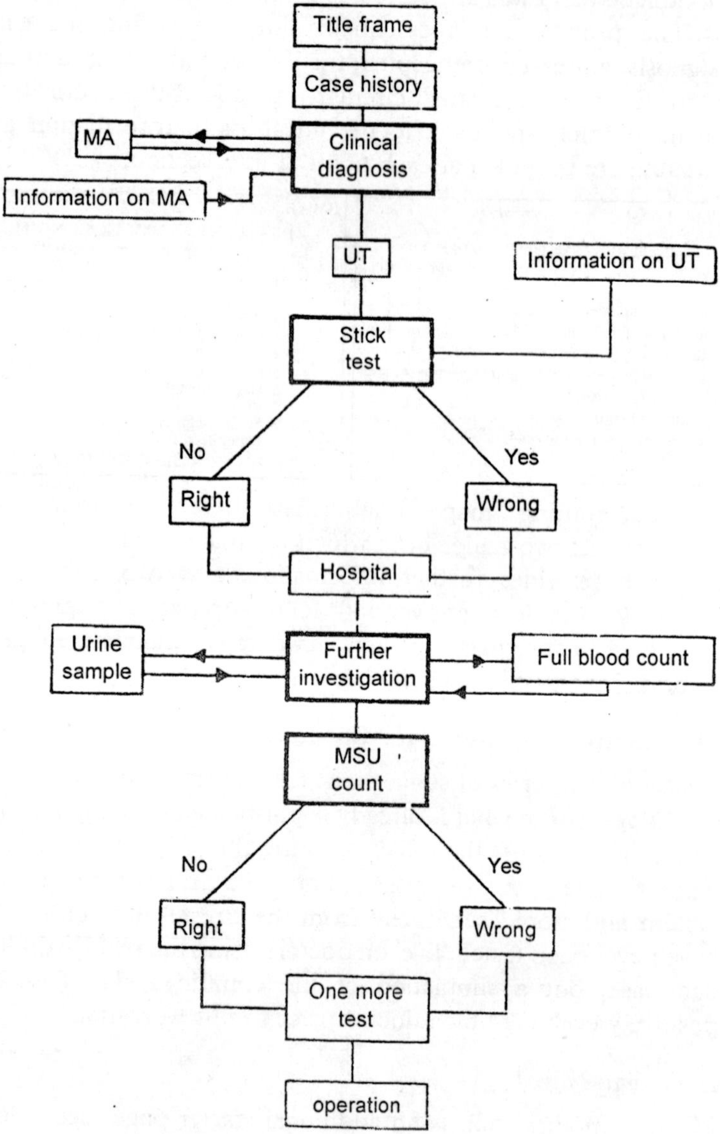

Routing map for first half of the case study.

study, they can dip into 10 or so selected pages to get a 'flavour' of the study and examine a few of the questions to be asked. They can then choose either to proceed or to abandon the case study. And finally, a busy doctor can simply skin to the concluding pages to take away the main points of the study. My additional starter page also indicates an overall aim, and gives the potential learner an idea of the time the case study will take to complete.

SCET 44504b Op

This case study is designed to test a doctor's knowledge of fever-related diagnosis in a child.

It will take between 20 – 30 minutes to complete.

KEY 1 TO START

KEY 2 TO SAMPLE THE PROGRAMME

KEY 3 TO SEE MAIN CONCLUSIONS.

10:46: 18

Additional Pages 2 and 3

My next additional pages (see below) come before the doctor is forced to make a decision about the likely clinical diagnosis. Here, I have added the option of seeing a summary of Dr. Andrew's findings. The doctor can view these and then return to the previous page to make his choice.

SCET 44504c Op

WHAT IS THE LIKELY CLINCAL DIAGNOSIS?

1. Urinary Tract infection.
2. Appendicitis
3. Mesenteric Auenitis
4. Virus Infection
5. Other febrile condition of children, e.g. middle ear infection or phenmonia
6. An Exanthema

KEY NUMBER ACCORDING TO YOUR CHOICE OR KEY TO SEE A SUMMARY OF DR ANDERWS FINDINGS

10:46:24

SCET 44504d Op

SUMMARY OF DR ANDERWS' FINDINGS

(A) Child vomited, no diarrhoea
(B) Urine "strong cloudy and smelly"
(C) Previous milder attacks
(D) Temp 40°C; pulse : 140
(E) Rebound tenderness in the right loin

KEY : TO MAKE YOUR CHOICE OF DIAGNOSIS

10:47: 08

Additional Pages 4 and 5

Each 'wrong' choice is the original case study allows the doctor the option of receiving further information about that particular diagnosis. These information pages use blue text to distinguish them from the main case study routing which is in yellow.

I have amended this process (see below) to allow the additional follow-up facility of references. The example I use is the choice of mesenteric adenitis as a likely diagnosis in the early part of the case study. The doctor is given some information about mesenteric adenitis and then given a choice between returning to the diagnosis page, looking at more information on other conditions, or looking at three mesenteric adenitis references.

SCET 44504e Op

MESENTERIC ADENITIS

Mesenteric adenitis is much more common in children than in adults.
It presents with a subumbilical colic. Pain is fleeting and not often localised occasionally at iliac fossa.
Mesenter is adenitis may be preceded by an upper respiratory tract infection.
The white cell count is often normal.
Mesenteric Adenitis is probably viral in origin.

Mesenteric Adenitis References-Key 2
To make a revised choice of the likely clinical diagnosis-Key 1
For info an other conditions Key 8 10:47:32

SCET 44504f Op

MESENTERIC ADENITIS IN CHILDREN

M.A. 1 Ironside AG: Survey of Infantile Adenitis Br. Med J 1970; iii; 20-4
M.A. 2 Bairagi R: On Validity of some Anthropometric Indicators as Predictors of m.a. Am J Clin Nutr 1981 : 74 : 2592-4
M.A. 3 Fry ENS: Continuous Narcotic Infusions for relief of m.a. Br. Med J 1979; 1; 1149
To order copies of articles, Key 1
To make a revised choice of likely clinical diagnosis, Key 2
Case study after diagnosis, key 3 10:46:16

The references I have selected are wholly fictitious, but they illustrate the interactive possibilities of the medium. If doctors found one or more of the references useful they could key in a response page and order a copy of the article(s) via Prestel. The same facility could be offered for each optional diagnosis and any particular doctor could be limited to an order of a maximum of, say, three or five articles. A small page charge could be levied for this to cover postage, if that was felt appropriate.

Additional Pages 6 and 7

When the child is admitted to hospital, the case study lists seven investigations and asks the doctor to pick out those of some value. In fact, this is a simple loop in the programme because they are all of value and the doctor is asked to look at them in turn.

I propose a slightly different procedure, where the doctor is first asked to list on paper a few investigations before, on keying 1, the complete list of seven appears.

Further information is then offered on each one.

In one sense it does not matter at all whether doctors do list the investigations on paper. The process will make them think

SCET 44504h Op

AT THE HOSPITAL

The Surgical Registrar confirms the History and Physical examination

Could you list (on paper) any further investigations which could help at this stage?

?

KEY 1 WHEN YOU ARE READY TO PROCEED

10:48:35

SCET 44504i Op

There are at least 7 investigations of some value. For further information about each one, key the relevant number:

1. Full blood count
2. Midstream urine sample
3. Serum urea and electrolytes
4. X-ray of chest
5. X-ray of abdomen
6. Blood culture
7. Supra-public aspiration of bladder

An MSU (more than 50 white and more than 50 red cells per cubic mm) confirms the presence of a urinary intect infection.

IAGREE - keys: IDISAGREE - key 9 10:49:18

about the issue and therefore react more positively to the list supplied in the next page.

Additional Page 8

With a book, the reader has a clear indication of progress merely by glancing at the pages already covered and the pages left to read. An electronic programme does not offer that facility, so some kind of sign-posting is necessary.

I insert a 'congratulations' page, which also gives the learner a choice between continuing through the case study, skipping to the concluding pages, or leaving the programme at that point.

SCET 44504k Op

CONGRATULATIONS

You are now half-way through this case-study.

Key 1 to continue

Key 2 if you would simply like the concluding frames.

If you would like to leave the programme at this point please note *445047 # to return to this frame.

10:49:34

The half-way marker can be flagged in many different ways. My method is only one option. But is important that there should be suitable markers inserted at regular intervals in the progeamme.

References

Rekkedal, T. (1973), *Innsendingsoppgarene i brevundervisningen*. NKI, Oslo, Norway.

Baath, John A. and Mansion, Nik-Ove (1977), *CADE — A System for Computer Assisted Distance Education.* Hermods Skola, Malmo, Sweden.

Anandam, Kamala (1976), *RSVP: A Guide for Implementia.* Miami-Dade Community College, USA.

Lewis, R. (1982), *How to Write Self Study Material.* CET, London, England.

5

Training Technologies

Background Note

At the same time as the conference, SCET mounted a two-day exhibition (TT83) designed to show some of the latest developments in training technologies. The council hoped that this exhibition would escape from the tired repetitions of the latest refinement of the flip-chart or yet another redesigned plastic case for the 16mm projector, and give instead a view of the applications of materials, machines and methods to the needs of training today and for the immediate future. Each potential exhibitor was therefore given an outline of the themes of the conference and a statement of the objectives of the exhibition. The resulting selection of exhibits cannot be claimed as completely representative of the main trends in development but it still provided interesting indications of progress.

New Wine in Old Bottles, or the Same Old Vinegar?

By the beginning of the week of the exhibition, 44 exhibitors had signed up and paid for space. The was well in excess of expectations. A third hall had been opened and a considerable waiting list of companies had eventually to be turned away. On that count alone the exhibition was a success. In the two days, more than 1000 people visited the exhibition. Add to that those attending the conference, who all took the opportunities provi-ded to visit TT83, and one has an attendance figure that would be the envy of many another educational technology exhibition.

Though from the point of view of quantity TT83 was visibly successful, it was a harder job to determine whether it had succeeded in terms of quality. The organisers had hoped that setting out objectives as they had done would influence the presentations so that there would be a genuine display of the technologies of training. The distance between London and Scotland can be measured in years, and many in education and training north of the border complain vociferously that exhibitions rarely venture further north than the Birmingham International Exhibition Centre. On a population basis, one in ten of the educational exhibitions should be in Scotland, or so they claim. Therefore, almost any exhibition would have been welcomed. The harder test was to see what was to be shown as representative of forward thinking in training technologies.

As the exhibitors arrived on the day before the opening, the organisers watched with curiosity as one small firm placed a dish antenna on the lawn in front of the building. A cable was run in through a window and connected to a flat box under a television set. Once this had been switched on, the small crowd that had gathered were greeted with pictures directly from Moscow. That nobody could understand what was being said did not seem important - that it was possible was all. It was some time before anybody asked what use it was to have pictures from Moscow.

Though this demonstration of satellite television was one of the major 'hits' of the exhibition, it was clearly a case of a delivery system looking for a worthwhile message to send. Time after time groups would gather and wonder at the quality of the images for several minutes before beginning to ask questions about its usefulness. Discussion would eventually get round to the potential of the European satellites for delivering material but there was little knowledge available as to how this would affect training. Mildly entertaining dross from a satellite probably won't look any different from the same dross broadcast in the conventional manner.

At the end of the same hall another exhibitor was demonstrating the ability to project large, bright television pictures on to a flat wall. Whether they were showing broadcast pictures or playback from a tape, one was impressed not so much by the quality of the images, which was surprisingly good, but by the effort to get back to something that looked like film. It appears that manufacturers are responding to genuine demand for bigger, better video images. There was no evidence, however, that the result would be any different from the passive reception of film.

Stand-holders in other halls were rigging projectors and computers, video-cameras and recorders. The learning materials were slower to emerge. The stands of companies giving advice and guidance looked sadly bare at this stage, suggesting that the worst fears of the educationalist were to be confirmed as hardware technology raced ahead of the provision of suitable software.

Balance

By the time the exhibition opened, however, the dominance of the machine had somewhat diminished and it was worth taking a more accurate count of what was being offered.

For this count a number of arbitrary subjects were chosen, derived not from the way in which the compaines described themselves (see list of exhibitors) but from what was actually presented on their stands.

The largest group were those producing or distributing audio-visual materials. Fourteen of the 44 companies were showing products designed mainly for the post-school training market. Of these the bulk were in the form of film and video-tape, though there was a noticeable trend towards multi-media packages designed specifically for particular learning methods, such as individualised learning, simulation exercises, and so on. It was perhaps disappointing that, despite the relatively long history of alternative methods of learning, there is still so little evidence that recognition of them has begun to penetrate the commercial market. Most of the films and video-tapes remain essentially traditional in style. The didactic mode of the training film has been to some extent modified by the comic genus of Cleese and other top actors, but the message is still packaged for delivery to a passive audience. In many cases it is just the wrapping that has changed, though some at least now state their objectives, which is a small advance.

Such films and video-tapes are unlikely to meet the individual and changing needs of industry and training, if the indications given by the main speakers at the conference are to be believed. At the moment, however, the style of the films is probably a fair reflection of the training methods used by the majority of companies, particularly for management training.

Some faith in the production industry's ability to respond to change is encouraged by the second largest category of exhibitor: nine of the 44 offered advice and training courses. Sometimes the same companies that sold films were prepared to produce learning materials tailored to the specific needs of clients, and to produce them in small quantities.

The sample was too small to draw any hard conclusions, but it did appear to back up other indications that there may be a growing place in the educational and training market for small companies. In the past, small producers have had a rough time competing against the major companies. Films or other media for broad-based audiences, such as middle management or safety training officers, had to be able to capture a large market, and this was best achieved by companies with a marketing and sales structure. The small firm hardly got a look in. With the advent of newer styles of learning and the prospect of a methodological lead from the Open Tech, trainers may be more ready to turn to the small company which with small overheads, can produce in short runs at a competitive rate. Some of these smaller companies are already making their mark because they have people at their heads who are well versed in newer methodologies - people who can construct new learning models - in other words, educational experts rather than producers or salesmen.

Better Hardware, Better Software?

The next largest group were those companies selling audio-visual hardware. These are the companies with the impressive stands, the shining cameras and projectors and the sparkling screens. Behind all the trimmings not much was new, though in fairness novelty is not everything, and here improvement to existing ranges seemed to be the order of the day. Film and slide projectors become more refined and easier to use (but harder to clean, and it is almost impossible with some to use only the middle section of a film). The changes are rung on the basic slide-tape projector, now that more and more packages are appearing in this format. Video equipment, however, shows some of the greatest changes. With advances in chip technology, the price of equipment like editing machines, time-base correctors, synch-pulse generators and a whole range of digital storage machines has plummeted in real terms bringing machines within the reach of institutional units which were not so long ago the preserve of broadcasters and big production companies. All this increases the potential for technical improvement to the appearance of video programmes. Whether new equipment will help raise the pedagogical standard is another question, the answer to which may depend on the willingness of companies to employ the right sort of people to make the programmes.

Big screen television projection is impressive but, despite the remarkable quality that can be achieved with some of the systems, it remains an uneasy compromise between film and conventional television reply. Beause of its technical limitations, television demands that only a small number of people watch any one set. At the same time, it is cheap to make copies from and often easier to handle than film. As a result, we are struggling to make the television picture as big as the old film image, so that large groups of people can sit and receive messages which like as not originated on film. Have we really advanced much in the way that we are using video? This is not the place to pursue the argument, but if the technological advances exhibited here were anything to go by we are still going round the same circle.

Five of the exhibitors displayed computers and four showed the specific use of computers in training. Given the title of the exhibition, many more computer manufacturers and distributors might have been expected. The audience was certainly more interested in the applications of the machines and in the software developed for them than in the number of small ingenious things that could be found inside the boxes. The relative lack of jargon surrounding these computers was refreshing: here at last were people prepared to think about materials that could serve the new style of learner; here were supports to open learning systems; here were courses based on computer programmes.

While some of the companies were showing highly specific training games and simulations, other programmes left the observer wondering as to their purpose to know that one can make a computer produce pretty pictures is not necessarily to understand the potential applications of that facility. Two companies demonstrated systems of coursework marking and assessment. Though this is not in itself new, the low cost of such equipment and programmes now brings them within the reach of many institutions. Robot arms controlled by microcomputers moved endlessly in a small scale reminder of what is already happening in industry - one of the developments that create the need for much of the other media in the exhibition.

Interactive Video, Where Were You?

Many of the visitors confessed themselves disappointed with the virtual absence of interactive video. It was the subject of one of the seminar groups and most people were aware from the educational press that interactive video was being hailed as a breakthrough in training technology. Efforts had been made to have more systems demonstrated, but only Sony had turned up with their Responder system. In this, a limited number of days on a board which hold the printed courseware allow variable access to a video-tape. Effective interaction with video-disc is eagerly awaited, but the wait is likely to be a long one for many sectors of training and education until the technical systems are sorted out and the economics of disc production become clear.

If learners in the near future are to have the opportunity to opt in and out of education as their personal needs arise, if learning is to take place away from lock-step institutional settings, and if IT82 had any influence at all, there was a need for a greater presence of communications technology. Disappointingly, only three exhibitors were displaying or using viewdata or Prestel in any form. Here again the exhibitors have the impression that this technology has not yet discovered how to match itself of learning needs. Though equally, perhaps, educationalists and trainers have not yet thought how they might best exploit it.

Throughout the two days of the exhibition, the television pictures from Russia had come cleanly in. To the viewer not understanding the language, there always appear to be more talking heads on other people's television. The Russians seemed indefatigable talkers and the visitors were undefeated watchers and listeners. A sterile technology waiting like a laboratory dish for the right cultural spores to be placed upon it remained the star attraction of the exhibition.

An audience survey conducted among exhibitors and visitors, while perhaps not very scientific, gave a strong impression that most were very happy to have had such an exhibition in Scotland. It may be that the very novelty gave the response an uncritical cast and, if so, this should be a signal to many more people than just SCET to get the messages to people who live outside London a bit more frequently. But despite the satisfaction expressed, this writer for one is left with a slight unease about the weight of traditional media in an exhibition supposed to look to he future. Despite all the excellent films, videos and other audio-visual media that were on view, only a minority of items seemed to have started with the needs of the learner. Too often there was a strong sense that marketing took precedence over everything else. Needs were incidental. Technology had made something possible so now it must be marketed. Films and videos were being sold because that is what those companies did. Such harsh criticism is not deserved by all the exhibitors, but those who placed the needs of the client more highly than the gloss on their product were in the minority.

The Gap to be Bridged

At a time when rapid change is affecting both education and training, and when may accepted methods and practices are being revolutionised, there are two great chasms between the needs of the learner and the ideas of those who produce the goods. First, few producers seem to be aware of or willing to move towards the emerging methods. Second, while many institutions do attempt to produce materials designed to meet user needs, they rarely achieve the quality o, production that is the norm for the commercial companies.

Perhaps presentation of the traditional is an accurate reflection of the methods currently entrenched in training, but to borrow a phrase used earlier in this book, an industry founded upon and using traditional technologies is a dying industry. Producers of learning materials and of the machines needed to display them need to respond to changes in methodology if there is not to be a serious mis-match between available resources and the needs of learners over the next few years. The effects of this particular new technology, that of educational methods, might have just as devastating an effect on the traditional audio-visual production industry as the new microchip technology is reported to be having on the traditional manufacturing industries of this country.

TT83–List of Exhibitors

The following are the exhibitors (in alphabetical order) and some of the items they each displayed.

Andrew Antennas

Lochgelly, Fife KY5 9HG
Tel: 0592 780561
A system of direct reception of television from foreign countries via space satellites. Britain and Russia already have satellites in operation, and it will soon be possible to receive television via satellite from France, Germany, Scandinavia, etc.

BBC Enterprises Ltd.

Educational and Training Sales, Room 508, Villiers House, London W5 2PA Tel.: 01-743 8000 ext 8301
Video-cassettes and 16mm films for sale from a catalogue of over 2000 BBC television programmes (including *The Computer Programme, Silicon Factor and Making the Most of the Micro).*

Bell & Howell AV Ltd.

Alperton House, Bridgewater Road, Aklperton, Wembley, Middlesex HA0 1EG
Tel.: 01-903 5411
A selection of audio-visual hardware, including in particular the Ringmaster 2 series of sound/slide projectors, ranging from a

simple playback unit to a multi-function, microprocessor-controlled programmable, record, edit, playback model.

BNA Communications Europe

17 Dartmouth Street, London SW1H 9BL
Tel.: 01-222 8834
New examples on video and slide-tape of management, supervisory, sales and safety training programmes (e.g. *Preventive Discipline,* and a programme on back injury prevention).

Brathay Training Opportunities

Brathay Hall, Ambleside, Cumbria LA 22 0PH
Tel.: 09663 3041
Information on a range of development courses provided at Brathay Hall for managers, supervisors and trainees for those positions. Courses, run in small groups, take the form of practical indoor and outdoor projects and group discussion.

British Council (Media Group)

10 Spring Gardens, London SW1A 2BN
Tel.: 01-930 8466
Information on the work of the Media Group in developing the use of the media, audio-visual aids and information technology in the British Council's educational services (several of which operate as part of the British aid programme to developing countries). The Group produces a quarterly journal, *Media in Education and Development,* which projects British experience within the framework of activity in many countries.

Cameron Video Systems

Burnfield Road Glasgow G46 7 TH
Tel.: 041-633 0077
A wide range of video equipment, including the Barcovision large screen projector.

Certified Accountants Educational Trust

PO Box 244, London WC2A 3 FF
Tel.: 01-242 6855 ext 251

Information on the range of services to industry and commerce offered by the Trust, and details of the internationally recognised Certified Diploma in Accounting and Finance.

Control Data Ltd.

77 Wells Street, London W1P 3RE
Tel.: 01-637 2171
A demonstration of the CDC 110 microcomputer (PLATO terminal and flexible disc drive), which enables students to take courses where and when convenient, independent of communication lines. The CDC 110 can also be used with the addition of a slave flexible disc drive to develop customers' own courseware. Also, information on computer courses run at six regional centres or in-house to meet customers' specific needs.

CRS Audio Visual Engineers

352 Nuneaton Street, Glasgow G40
Tel.: 041-554 2161
A range of audio-visual equipment available for hire or sale, including the Videocube, a compact portable video-cassette/ television unit.

CST Training Resources Ltd.

78 High Street, Bushey, Herts WD2 3DE
Tel.: 01-950 5003
Information on CST's individual design and production service for vidocassette, films and slide-tape training programmes, and on their library of video training programmes for hire or purchase.

Educational Video Index Ltd.

25 Thurloe Street, London SW7 2LH
Tel: 01-581 8733
Educational and training video programmes available from EVI's catalogue of approximately 400.

Employment Relations Resource Centre

62 Hills Road, Cambridge CB2 1LA
Tel.: 0223 315944

Information on ERL's advisory services on improving industrial relations and on planning and choice of materials for organisation-based training programmes to this end. Also, course materials produced by ERL and available for hire or sale.

Glasgow College of Technology

Cowcaddens Road, Glasgow G4 0BA
Tel.: 041-332 7090 ext. 311
Information on management, word-processing and computing courses and advisory services available to industry and commerce, including a demonstration of viewdata facilities.

Human Resource Associates

18th Floor, St. Alphage House, Fore Street, London EC2Y 5DA
Tel.: 01-638 4264
A range of self-directed learning materials to inculcate the right attitudes. Skills and knowledge to help people make the best use of new technology. Also, details of a consultancy service on the use of technology for more effective communication.

IBM United Kingdom

21 St. Andrew Square, Edinburgh EH2 1AE
Tel.: 031-556 9292
The new IBM Personal Computer (for individuals, small business and education) and the IBM System/23, also for small businesses. Also, the Displaywriter, a text processing system with built-in dictionary to highlight typing errors.

Institute of Supervisory Management

22 Bore Street, Lichfield, Staffordshire WS13 6LP
Tel.: 05432 51345
Information on the Institute's formal and diploma courses in supervisory management, and about its short courses on Current Legislation. Store-keeping, Maintenance Supervision, etc.

International Tutor Machines Ltd.

15 Holder Road, Aldershot, Hampshire GU12 4PU
Tel.: 02582 28512

The Portascribe overhead projection, the new Unigraph 2000 (combined 35mm and overhead projector). And the Unanimate Presentation Aid (combined portable writing board, flip-chart stand, projection screen, drawing board, lectern and table).

Jordanhill College of Education

Southbrae Drive, Glasgow G13 1PP
Tel.: 041-959 1232
Productions from the Audio-Visual Media Department (including computer generated graphics from the IBM 4331 mainframe computer), and information about pre-service and in-service courses in Educational Technology and Media Studies.

Kendata Peripherals Ltd.

Nutsey Lane, Totton, Southampton SO4 3NB
Tel.: 0703 869922
A range of systems based on Longines Optical Mark Readers to automate the administration of multiple choice examinations and student assessment schemes. Systems can include output and storage facilities or will interface with a separate computer. Commercial and industrial applications include payroll variations, stock control, etc.

Kermack Electronics

112-24 Woodlands Road, Glasgow G3 6HB
Tel.: 041-332 2036
Video-disc display. Also information on video and audio equipment available for sale or hire, and on associated design, installation, maintenance and tape copying services.

Link Electronics Ltd.

North Way, Andover, Hampshire SP 10 5AJ
Tel.: 0264 61345
First public demonstration in the UK of the new General Electronic TALARIA video-projector.

Management Games Ltd.

11 Woburn Street, Ampthill, Bedford MK45 2HP
Tel.: 0525 404248

Exercises for participative management training, including computerised simulation/games, case studies, selection tests and programmes on interpersonal skills.

McMillan Video Ltd.

Unit 3, Lindsay Street, Arbroath DD11 1RP
Tel.: 0241 78411
A wide range of video equipment for sale, plus details of advice and repair services, and of mobile demonstrations around Scotland.

Melrose Film Productions Ltd.

8-12 Old Queen Street, London SW11H 9HP
Tel.: 01-222 1744
Videos and films, with associated documentation for management training. Topics include Project Management, Computer Security, Number Skills, and the use of audio-visual aids.

Microcom
Microcomputing (Scotland) Ltd.

89 West Camphell Street, Glasgow G2 6SE
Tel.: 041-204 0812/3
Commodore microcomputers and educational software available from Microcom, plus information on service to education and to business.

Microelectronics Educational Development Centre

Paisley College of Technology, High Street, Paisley PA1 2BE
Tel.: 041-887 0962
Display of microcomputers. Information on MEDC's advice and training services to business, industry and post-school education in Scotland. Also, details of publications, including *Micronotes* (series on applications) and *Microfiles* (current activities throughout the UK).

Millbank Films Ltd.

Thames House North, Millbank, London SW1P 4QG
Tel.: 01-834 4444

Management training programmes on Health and Safery, Security, Financial Awareness, etc.

National Computing Centre Ltd.

Anderston House, 389 Argyle Street, Glasgow G2 8LR
Tel.: 041-204 1101
Training materials and guides on computer language, concepts, and skills, *Computing for Managers, How to Choose your Small Business Computer,* office use of information technology, etc.

National Extension College

18 Brooklands Avenue, Cambridge CB2 2HN
Tel.: 0223 316644
New computer marking system 'MAIL' (Micro Aided Learning), for use on a BBC microcomputer, produces diagnostic letters for individual students and maintains student records. Also, course materials for the BBC microcomputer and materials linked to Channel 4 Adult Numeracy and Small Business Education programmes.

ODI Ltd.

Old Road, Shotover Hill, Headington, Oxford OX3 8TA
Tel.: 0865 67171
Information on management and organisation development programmes and consultancy services, including the development of in-house, videobased programmes.

Open University in Scotland

60 Melville Street, Edinburgh EH3 7HF
Tel.: 031-226 3851
Multi-media courseware and assessment material, plus demonstrations of Cyclops computer-aided tuition and of viewdata.

Outward Bound Loch EiL Ltd.

Loch Eil, Achdalieu, Fort William, Inverness-shire PH33 7NN
Tel.: 03977 320
Information on Outward Bound action-centred development courses run outside Fort William.

Paisley College of Technology

67 High Street, Paisley PA1 2BE
Tel.: 041-887 1241

Practical Technology Ltd.

112 Cornwall Street South, Glasgow G41 1AA
Tel.: 041-427 5364
SAM - Sequence Action Monitor - a solid state electronic solution to the circuit design problem encountered when pneumatic actuators are required to operate a predetermined sequence. The wiring out procedure needs to be carried out only once, and the sequence and all subsequent changes are effected by means of software alone.

PTS (Electronics) Ltd.

Middleton Hall, Uphall, Edinburgh EH52 5DH
Tel.: 0506 854857
A range of video systems.

Rank Aldis Training Films and Video

PO Box 70, Great West Road, Brentford, Middlesex TW8 9HR
Tel. 01-568 9222
Management training films on subjects including sales, industrial relations, safety and communication.

Scotia Office Machines

2-4 Castle Terrace, Edinburgh EH1 2DP
Tel.: 031-229 2261
Educational dictating system using the Wollensak cassette duplicator and Sanyo dictating and transcription machines. Also, a range of magnetic media for computer input, and information on technical support services for DISKY and other products.

Scotwork Ltd.

128 Hope Street, Glasgow G2 2TG
Tel.: 041-204 2186

Information on Scotwork's personnel consultancy services and negotiating skills courses run in Scotland, England and abroad.

Service Training Ltd.

34 The Square, Kenffworth, Warwickishire CV8 1EB
Tel.: 0926 512421
The Slidemagic Nikon F3 pin-registered camera system, available for hire or purchase, and audio-visual programmes on catering and book-keeping. Also, information on Service Training's consultancy and wide-ranging audio-visual production service.

Sony UK Ltd.

Pyrene House, Sunbury-on-Thames, Middlesex TW16 7AT
Tel.: 09327 89581
Demonstrations of the Sony Video Responder interactive video systems.

Supervisory Management Training Ltd.

21 Green Lane, London SE20 7JA
Tel. 01-778 1661
Ready to use and tailor-made training packages, and a demanstration of telephone training equipment, 'Teletrainer.'

Tecquipment International Ltd.

Bonsall Street, Long Eaton, Nottingham NG10 2AN
Tel.: 06076 62611
Demonstration of a microcomputer controlled 'robor' arm. Information on a range of products and service in the design and manufacture of 'hands-on' teaching equipment for engineering (including electronics and telecommunications) at all levels.

Teltale Ltd.

1 Bensham Lane, Croydon, Surrey CR0 2RU
Tel.: 01-689 6824
Information on educational programmes, documentary and fiction films and video, for supply to satellite television

companies, institutions and domestic users. Also, information on programmes for use in computer education.

Tyne Video (Scotland) Ltd.

22 Albion Way, Kelvin Industrial Estate, East Kilbride G75 0YH
Tel: 03552 48131
New Series Five U-Matic video-recorders and a range of viewdata terminals and printers. Information on a variety of other equipment available for purchase, and on Tyne Video's after sales service.

6

Reshaping of Technical Education

What we notice in the country today is that about 45 per cent people are living below the poverty line; there is a rampant unemployment on one hand and shortage of skilled and knowledgeable people on the other; brain drain is increasing; there is an excess of import than export, leading to unfavourable Balance of Payments; per capita income is only U.S. 360 which is one of the lowest in the world; the share of India in world market in spite of abundant natural resources, and huge population (16 per cent) is less than 1 per cent; in hi-tech products contribution in insignificant, the economic and indust-rial recession is leading to spiraling prices; large number of industries are sick, locking up huge capital and throwing people out of jobs; capacity utilisation and productivity in industry is far too low.

Solutions to these and many more problems in this age of science and technology are to be found partly in improving in quality and quantity of "Technical Education". Education in general and technical in particular has so far failed, the nation and hence is the pressing need of its revamping.

Science and Technology Matters Most

With the adoption of five year plan approach to development the need of developing "Scientific and Technological Capability" of people has become critical. The limiting factor for growth now is not the availability of physical and financial resources, hard work, sincerity and enthusiasm, but it is the application of science and technology in various vocations and professions. There are revolutionary changes in developed countries in technology generation and technical education to masses. It is largely on account of these that we the people in India and also people in other developing countries, are getting economic shocks. This ought to be perceived in proper perspective and corresponding changes in technical education in our country be carried out. So long as they are not done our economy will remain in difficulty. This is a writing on the wall which we have to read. According to AKIO MORITA Chairman of Sony Corporation, "If we want modern industry tomorrow, we have to have modern universities today. The economic stagnation is a result of stagnation in engineering academic institutions."

Hence is the necessity of revamping of technical education, and this seminar.

Changing World: Capacity to Cope with

The whole world is seeking change, so we must also change. Our institutions, their organisation structures, systems and procedures, which although at one time have served will, no more suit the purpose today. They must be improved to enable us to cope with the changing world.

With the increased facility of communication globalisation of market, internationalism in trade and commerce, migration of human and intellectual capital is tending to become the order of the day. Competition is no more domestic and regional but it is global. So as to prepare the youths for such competitive environment, the technical education institutions and the teachers in particular, ought to posses Global Vision and Global Attitudes.

Producing just simple engineers now is not enough. Our technical education institutions now would have to turn out engineers competent by world standards. This demands world class institutes and teachers. Do our systems permit them to be so. If not our systems need to be altered.

Problems

The following problems invite our immediate attention.

Today, the teachers and institutes have less of opportunities to be in touch with innovations in developed world; Libraries are in bad shape; the curricula are irrelevant and outdated; examination system is too bulky and consumes too much time; leaving less time for learning; institutes have become teaching shops and do not involve in research; lessons of entrepreneurship are not given to students; teaching area is not attractive, and positions of teaching are vacant; institute industry interaction is lacking; peoples demand on technical education is not met with.

It is now necessary to examine such problems scientifically, dispassionately and evolve solutions, and strategies for their implementation. Precisely for this purpose the conference is being held.

It is reported by New Education Policy, 1986, that the education should be more responsive to the industrial needs and the aspirations of youths, for which the education commission has recommended grant of Autonomy to Colleges. Unfortunately, so far not a single college in Maharashtra State has been granted autonomy. Why? The seminar should address this question, and impress upon Government its urgent need.

Continuing Engineering Education programmes in colleges and polytechnics are prescribed by NEP (1986), so as to improve the productivity of practising engineers and to improve the production immediately. Engineering Colleges, have three legitimate missions namely, teaching, research and community service. But they are largely doing only teaching and that too poorly. The other two missions of research and community service are neglected.

Research, Entrepreneurship, Continuing Engineering Education are well outlined by NEP, but they are not implemented. Neither the Government nor the institutes are serious about their implementation. Probably a determined attempt through a task force needs to be made. The seminar delegates may identify the steps for vigorous implementation.

Foreign aid is being obtained to modernise the institutions at polytechnic and college levels. It is very much necessary, but to make most of it, it must be preceded by restructuring of institutions and revising the systems and procedures. It is the teachers who probably have to take more active hand in bringing about the changes. It is they who have to impress upon the

Government, as to how damaging it is to public interest, if revamping is not done on time.

It is hoped that the seminar delegates will discuss, debate the problems and evolve solutions, and strategies to implement them.

Whose Responsibility?

The Government has a central role to play in revamping of technical education.

The following deserve to be considered on priority.

- Autonomy to deserving Government/aided/private engineering colleges/polytechnics be granted.
- Separate Engineering universities be established forthwith.
- Continuing Engineering Education courses be started in each College/Polytechnics.
- Entrepreneurship Technology Parks be set up with any loss of time.
- Budget allocation to technical institutes be increased, for cost of not spending on education in higher.
- Post Graduate and research education be given fillip.
- Mobility of teachers and their exposure to developed world be promoted. Institutions should be made attractive enough.

Revamping of technical education does not need necessarily additional financial resources, although desirable. It needs a will to change with time, to give up inertia and cope up with changing world. It needs knowledge to identify activities of priority and allocate existing funds in a more rational manner. Revamping, in fact, releases funds form low productivity activities, in favour of high productivity activities.

The Government industry, institutions and teachers have to come together, step up the organisational capacity to prepare a joint plan for action for revamping of technical education and implement the same.

7

Perspectives of Technical Education

For the past few weeks there has been a detailed discussion on the National Policy for Education in the country on the basis a policy document Challenges of Education. The Prime Minister has expressed his views from various platforms on the need for meaningful change in the Educational Policy of the country to prepare its youth to face the twenty-first century. Among other things, the new concepts, as relevant to the field of technical education, are:

1. To develop human resources at appropriate level so that every person can earn his livelihood either through gainful employment or through self-employment.
2. To enable the youth to face the rapid changes in technology by providing adequate training so that they can learn, absorb and adapt to new horizons in technology in order to improve the productivity and production and meet the challenge of technically advanced countries.
3. To develop human resources in conformity with the heritage and environment of this country and convert these resources into assets for growth rather than liabilities of inadequately educated and improperly trained youth seeking jobs.

With these three broad concepts, it is necessary that technical education in the country is developed in close partnership with the industry and an interaction between institutions and industries is developed for their mutual benefit and for the larger benefit of the country.

The National Policy on education enunciated by the Government of India in 1986 aimed, *inter-alia*, at relating education more closely to the working life of people, a sustained and intensive effort to raise the quality of education and an emphasis on development of science and technology. These objectives when viewed from the point of view of technical education have a special significance. Those at the helm of affairs concerning technical education have the responsibility of organising this activity in such a manner that it will not only serve the needs of different industries but promote their growth and development today and in future. Towards this aim the academic institutions and the user industries must play the role of inseparable partners, the academic institutions have to function like a prime mover.

Several reports have been brought out on the concept of industry - Institution interaction and collaboration in the past. Among the various avenues suggested for such an interaction, the following seem to be rational and feasible: (a) Sandwich pattern of Technical Education, (b) Exchange of academic faculty and industrial experts, (c) Consultancy services offered by educational institutions, and (d) Adoption of institution by the industry.

Sandwich Pattern of Technical Education

Experiments in sandwich pattern of technical education have been carried out in the country for the past few years. This type of education has been favoured in several places in Europe and U. K. while in the U. S. A. similar systems are used under the name of Co-operative Education. Though several polytechnics and Engineering Colleges decided to embark upon the introduction of sandwich pattern of education, only a few have actually done so and continue successfully. The Victoria Jubilee Technical Institute, Shri Bhagubhai Mafatlal Polytechnic and Fr. Agnel Polytechnic in Bombay have to be credited for successful implementation of sandwich courses at the diploma level in several disciplines and also at the degree level in Production Engineering in Govt. College of Engineering, Pune since the mid-sixties and have improved the system to the benefit of the students.

The Industry in and around Bombay have welcomed the well trained practice-oriented engineers produced by these Institutions. Not only have these courses been found to be effective in the conventional disciplines of Civil, Mechanical and Electrical Engineering but for training in the field of diversified specialised disciplines such as Electronics, Production Engineering, Plastics Engineering, etc., sandwich courses have been found to be almost essential.

In the development of successful sandwich programmes, the academic institutions and participating industry have to be closely associated in every phase of planning and implementation. The planning phase would include curriculum development, choice of appropriate industries to impart in plant training, drawing up of detailed plans for effective use of the time spent by the student in the industry, deciding the manner in which the in-plant training should be assessed and so on. The implementation phase on the other hand, would involve the placement of students, effective supervision by both the academic tutor from the teaching institution and the industrial tutor from the industry, counselling the students prior to and during the period of industrial training, evaluation of the performance jointly by academic and industrial tutors and finally organising proper feedback to the authorities of both the institution and the industry so that necessary modifications can be effected in subsequent programmes.

In order to achieve success in all these phases of the system, it is most essential to have a good rapport between academic institution and the participating industry. It has been experienced in the past that in spite of good intention on the part of the authorities, the lack of rapport and motivation on the part of the two tutors can defeat the purpose of in plant training. It is essential, therefore that both academic institution and the involved industry should identity their respective tutors and arrange for mutual beneficial meetings from time to time, so that the training and supervision is effective. Motivation of two tutors is indeed a difficult task and can be brought about only if the tutors are fully convinced of their important role and thus are totally committed to their task.

The purpose of in-plant training is manifold. Apart from exposing the students to the industrial environment, developing practice-oriented attitudes and skills, the student is also expected to learn certain subjects both in theory and practice through industrial training. It is clear that subjects like Manufacturing Process and Plant Maintenance, Surveying Practive Drafting Practice, Quantity Surveying, etc. can be better learnt during in-plant training. With this background it is necessary to formulate the curriculum jointly by academic institutions and the industry in such a way that the requisite content of the syllabus is properly distributed to be learnt at both places. In other words, in-plant training is an integral part of the process of the teaching certain aspects of different subjects. Another important feature in the curriculum is the flexibility that is required to be built into it. It should be possible for the authorities to react to the changing needs of the industry, have joint discussions and effect quick changes in the content of the syllabus. Without such flexibility, the students are likely to lose the benefit of learning of technical advances made in the industry. Flexibility can be assured only through two major changes in the existing pattern of teaching and evaluation. Firstly, there must be full academic freedom for the institution to make adequate modifications in the course curriculum and secondly, the evaluation must be joint responsibility of both the academic institution and the industry and be carried out on continued basis.

If the sandwich course is to serve the teaching process, the industry must be willing to assign motivated industrial tutors for the job. The students must not be allowed to stay around and left to themselves to absorb whatever they can be more observation but should be properly guided through programmes, assignments and tasks which will have to be pre-planned. Persons in the industry are generally under a lot of pressure to ensure higher production at economically viable cost and are likely to feel that the presence of students taking in-plant training hampers their work. Further, they may be averse to the students taking up their valuable time. Though these reaction, are understandable, it is necessary to appreciate that participation in in-plant training programme is a long-term investment for the industry, rich dividends from which can be obtained by ensuring that only well-trained practice oriented engineers will enter the industrial world. Such a person will have developed proper supervisory skills in his chosen discipline and also in man-management. It may also be pertinent note that young students have at times offered a fresh unbiased approach to certain ticklish problems. The academic tutor also plays an important role in the supervision of in-plant training. Students must have access to their academic tutor very often to solve their technical and environmental problems.

Thus, it is seen that a well planned industry institution interaction through sandwich pattern can provide a meaningful insurance towards developing well trained practice oriented engineers.

Exchange of Academic Faculty and Industrial Experts

It has been said that there exists a considerable gap between what is taught at the academic institutions and what is required by an engineer in the industry. Though it is not possible for the academic institution to produce an engineer 'tailor made' to suit the requirements of a particular industry, it is certainly possible for the institutions to incorporate in the curriculum, training leading to industry orientation and transfer of knowledge regarding the recent developments. The expertise and capabilities of executives, managers and technical personnel from the industry; research institutions and professional bodies can be utilised for supplementing the capabilities of the academic institutions by creating certain posts of 'Adjunct Professors' Enlightened industries could depute some of their leading technical personnel as 'Adjunct Professors' in institutions for a specific period. These Professors could be involved in delivering lectures on advanced practice oriented developments in the industry, help students to develop a proper industrial perspective, guide some of the final year students in their project work and associate themselfes with the academic personnel in development of new experimental systems to be taught to the students. Their presence in the institute would help generate confidence in the minds of the industry which will certainly appreciate the graduate student who has been taught in part by one of their kind. Such a person can also provide a nucleus for generation of new ideas for research in the minds of the academic personnel. It is known that in the western countries such as U.S.A. such 'Adjunct Professors' are available at leading Universities. *It is also possible for the 'Adjunct Professor' to know the capabilities of the academic faculty and bring to his industry on return. Certain new ideas from the academic world for the benefit of the industry itself.* The benefits of such a system are well known. Exploration of this concept with a few industries in Bombay revealed that even though the top management showed willingness to depute appropriate personnel, there appeared to be certain apprehension in the minds of the executives to accept this role. It is essential to have a proper dialogue and evolve methodology to promote the concept of 'Adjunct Professors' perhaps, part-time assignments on specific subject/projects on contract basis may be feasible.

A reverse system of placing an academic faculty member in the industry for a specific period is also worth a lot. Experiments in this direction have been made by providing Quality Improvement Programmes sponsored by Government of India whereby academic faculty members are placed in industry for a period of three months during their vacation. Experience of such personnel who have spent short time in the industry suggests that they stand to gain by their association with the industry personnel, are able to appreciate the problems of the industry, are in a position to converse and discuss technical problems with industry counterparts effectively and help themselves to tone up their teaching work. It is not uncommon to find that such Q.I.P. trained faculty members seem to be rejuvenated with their industrial experience and bring back into the academic institution a new flavour for industry oriented teaching.

Another avenue for getting benefit of the expertise in the industry is through the system of Visiting faculty for teaching specific topic in a subject. This is certainly possible in industrially developed areas, Experience of the institutions in Mumbai in this regard is encouraging.

Consultancy Services Offered by Educational Institutions

Several educational institutions possess a strong potential to offer consultancy services to different industries. The major strength of such institution comprise a keen and competent faculty, a wide range of testing facility, a well equipped library, high speed computing facilities and the possibility of evolving multi-disciplinary task force under one roof. The benefits of such consultancy activities are mutual. While the industry is able to get their problems solved for reasonable costs, the educational institutions are able to develop an industrially oriented knowledge base among the faculty and earn some revenue to helped partially their infrastructural developments. An indirect but relevant gain of the educational institutions is the opportunity to maintain rapport with the industry and tone up the teaching in the classroom.

The Indian Institutes of Technology, some of the Universities and certain engineering colleges have been engaged in consultancy activities. They can claim to have large private and public sector industries and also Governmental Departments as their clients, V.J.T.I. in Bombay for example, has undertaken consultancy projects for the Department of Atomic Energy, CIDCO, ONGC, Hindustan Petroleum, Bharat Petroleum, Hindustan Lever, Larsen & Toubro many more.

Consultancy projects that can be handled by institutions are varied in nature and every institution has to ascertain its capabilities in this field by assessing its resources in terms of manpower and equipment available. A very significant aspect of such projects is that they have to be time-bound and academic institutions must recognise their responsibility to deliver the goods in time. It is possible to classify consultancy projects in two categories. The first one would include handling problems involving analysis, testing, design and product development while the second world cover continuing education of industrial personnel. There is scope for all types of educational institutions of higher learning like I.I.Ts and engineering colleges offering post-graduate education as well as those offering undergraduate training and technician education to participate.

Problems in the first category of consultancy services can further be divided into three types. Firstly, some of the industries would prefer to assign tasks of routine analysis, testing and design. This may be required to be done either because these industries may face such problems infrequently and may not have adequate personnel or equipment at their disposal or because the problem may involve some complexities for which the educational institutions can provide testing or computational facilities. Perhaps, every engineering college can participate in tacking such problems. The second type problem faced by the industry is the one which can be identified by the industrial engineers but cannot be solved by them since the industry may not have its own R&D facility and would need consultation with academic engineers who have had the opportunity to keep abreast of the latest development through library research, guidance at post-graduate level and contacts with other similar industries. These types of problems could be handled by appropriate application of known methods and techniques adapted to suit the particular problem. All institutions of higher leaning and some engineering colleges having experienced and motivated faculty can participate in this activity. The third type of problem could be tackled by some institutions of higher learning as they would require basic and fundamental research. Problems of this kind may not be well defined and would require constant updating of problem definition as research progresses within the broad objectives. A typical example of such a problem is complex product development.

Thus, the educational institution has to judge its potential maintain a constant rapport with industrial units, particularly in the neighbourhood and develop the consultancy services. All such consulting projects should attract consultation fees and after deducting the expenditure involved, the balance should be shared between the institution and its participating faculty in a predetermined proportion. The funds thus collected should not be considered as a revenue for recurring expenditure of the Institute but should be used to build up a reserve fund for future development of the infrastructural facilities both in terms of the faculty and equipment.

Teaching technicians and technologists is the forte of educational institution. With the rapid growth in technology, the need for continuing education of industrial personnel cannot be overemphasised. Depending upon the level of training required, services of polytechnics, engineering colleges and institutions of higher learning can be utilised to develop structured programmes either at the institutions or 'in house' in the industry. S.B.M. Polytechnic in Bombay has been actively engaged in promoting such programmes for the Builders Association, Plastic Industry, etc.

Adoption of Institutions by Industry

The concept of adoption of institutions by industries was promoted by All India Council of Technical Education (AICTE) in 1976. It called upon Industry to be active partners in developing technical Institutions with assurance from the Government for support in conducting existing activities by meeting normal expenditure. The industry was thus asked to manage the Institution and provide resources for future expansion. Public sector Organisations were also asked to adopt INSTITUTIONS under this scheme. The concept aimed at bridging Theory Practice gap by bringing management expertise and infrastructural resources of Industry to Institutions. Despite attempts by many, for reasons will-known, no substantial progress could be achieved in this direction. However, a few examples of modified versions of 'Adoption' to a limited extent can be seen under operation, e.g.

1. An Industry supporting a specific programme at an Institution and involving itself in developing and monitoring the programmes. The support may be included in or providing resources, providing faculty. In-plant training facility and participating in curricular planning and evaluation.
2. Management of Academic Institution setting up an exclusive Industry and ensuring support to the institution out of income of the Industry. The industry would also organise training of students.
3. Management of Industry starting an independent Institution

for the conduct of technical courses and affiliating the same to the relevant Board of Technical examination.

Following cases for Maharashtra State are interesting.

a) M/s. Larsen & Toubro Ltd. have promoted Larsen & Toubro Institute of Technology (LTIT) on a planned basis and are conducting four year sandwich semester pattern courses. It has constituted a Governing Body as required by the Government of Maharashtra. Representatives of the Government, the Industry and other experts are thus providing guidelines and direction. Resources of M/s. Larsen & Toubro Ltd. are available to LTIT.

Flexibility of Approach

Adequate flexibility should be introduced in the working of the institutions by granting Autonomy to the deserving. Autonomy in the academic, administrative and financial spheres would go along way in developing the desired interactive. Academic Autonomy would provide avenues to effect quick changes and modifications in the curricula so as to respond to the changing needs of the industry. Administrative Autonomy would ensure prompt implementation of any changes and effective discharge of the institutional functions. Financial Autonomy can be made workable by sanctioning a rational grant for recurring expenditure on a per student per annum basis and permitting the Head of the Institution freedom to accommodate suitable changes to attain the educational goals. It is indeed an onerous task to run an Autonomous Institution and maintain credibility of performance but given the opportunity and inspired leadership, many academic institutions will not be found wanting. Autonomous Institutions should be subjected only to an Academic Audit by appropriate Committees with representatives both the Government and the industry.

8

Assessment of Institutes of Technical Education

It gives me great pleasure to welcome you all the distinguished delegates, the members of ISTE Maharashtra and Goa, who are present here in large number on this auspicious occasion of the first ISTE convention being held in Walchand College of Engineering, Sangli. The Section managing committee in its meeting held in Pune, made a decision to hold every year such a convention. This is with a view to address the "current issues in Technical Education" and to shape its future.

Walchand College of Engineering, Sangli is celebrating this year its Golden Jubilee, and during another meeting in Mumbai in the office of Director of Technical Education, Prof. P.A. Kulkarni, offered to host. We are very much happy that this college and other colleges in this region have made all the arrangements for our lodging, boarding, discussions and deliberations. We would like to complement, the organisers for very ably arranging for the convention.

This convention should mark the beginning of an effort to review and examine technical education policies and practices every year and offer its expert advice, feedback to Government, Universities, Industries associations and various other stake holders. The venue like the National ISTE convention is supposed to be shifting from institution to institution every year. Offers for the convention of next year are invited from institutions and the managing committee may decide in its meeting the venue for the next year.

Now the membership of ISTE in Maharashtra and Goa has gone to about 5500 in 217 Institutions. ISTE chapters in most of the institutions are quite active performing a number of activities like special lectures, competitions, industrial surveys, visits, etc. Students Chapters have also been set up and are still being set up. As a Chairman, I have been receiving reports almost every day from one or the other chapter, I would like to express high degree of satisfaction and convey to ISTE Head Quarter. Dr. P.J. George with pride that ISTE in Maharashtra has now taken off, and Maharashtra State with the support from DTE Prof. Chopane and the Government are attending to seriously address issues in technical education so as to make this State a "World Class" place for Technical Education.

I would like to appeal today to all the members who pay subscription from year to year to kindly become life members. We all already have been realising the advantages, that we get News-letter from Headquarter in our houses giving us valuable information about what is happening in the country, and the world in the field of Technical education. You can write and convey your feelings, impressions to all others through this media. I have no doubt that you will consider and choose to become life member.

Technical Education Provides Answer to Competitiveness

The real answer to competitiveness problem of the state and nation is education in general and Technical in particular. In this time of globalisation, and rapid technology change, what matters most is the technological ability of people.

Time has come to declare "Technical education" as a Singular Solution to the economic ills in this country. Let me humbly put it that we are highly deficient in Technology, practically starving for Innovation, and in these times of Globalisation, we have been importing and importing technology in spite of our high potential. Technical literacy, scientific and technological capability of masses is far too low. Time has come that private and Government Institutions both must now compare themselves to their counterparts in developed countries and know where we stand in Global comparison. We have to learn and even overtake them in respect of standard in education.

Restructuring Technical Education

U.S.A. has Silicon Valley, Japan has seventeen of them. Do we have the silicon valley approach to innovation? What technical education institutes are doing today to be competitive twenty years from now? We have started designing 9th Five Year Plan. It should include all above proven approaches. Education needs have now globalised and we must globalise to meet them. We have to think in big terms so as to convert a threat into opportunity. We have no doubt that jointly we all will be about to do this.

All this requires essentially a solid backing from Centre and State Governments. It the legitimate role and responsibility of ISTE members also to educate people to the importance of technical education. The budget of State Government for technical education is for too small. Government is planning to build India a Technology oriented nation. It wants to harvest new world wide opportunities arising out of new technologies. Development plans for industries, without matching investments, and matching strategies in technical education. We the members of ISTE would have to shout in the ears of planners, funding agencies and politicians that the limiting factor for economic growth today is technical education. A major change in funding of engineering education system is indeed the need of the hour.

A Call to Action

I was reading a report on Engineering Education from National Research Council of U.S.A. published in 1995. One of the main recommendation of this report which is relevant to us is as under.

Conduct Institutional Self-assessment

"To meet challenges that a nation faces in 21st Century each engineering college" school should enter a period of experimentation monitored by self-assessment and feed back from industry and all stake holders that are characterised by willingness to change and by open, active communication across the entire community. This process is likely to reveal many needed actions of institutional level and Government levels.

Are Private Institutes more Enterprising

It gives me great pleasure to welcome you all, the distinguished delegates from all over the country, from institutions, private and Government, of College and polytechnic levels, to this 25th Annual ISTE Convention being hosted by VRCE, Nagpur. We are very much delighted to have you with us to share concerns on technical education at a time when it is challenged most by world competitive environment. We, at this convention attempt to present to you a comfortable stay, and an atmosphere for fruitful debates and discussions on the theme chosen.

"Private Sector Participation in Technical Education and its Implications"

Privatisation of engineering education, in India, is a pretty old hat. But still a question is lingering in the minds of people whether privatisation is good? Question is also raised whether technical education in institutions managed and maintained by Government is adequate and can it cope with the present and future challenges? The system and procedures, management styles and strategies are undergoing drastic changes under external pressures.

Engineering in future will be challenged, as never before to shape the nature and quality of life in the twenty first century. Engineering education will be at the forefront of the effort to meet that challenges Engineering education in India will have to be highly adaptive to the demands of the FIVE YEAR PLANS, producing well rounded professional engineers to be able to work together efficiently in teams, to identify and solve complex problems in industry, academic, Government and society. Engineering in India, will have to compete well in regional, national as well as global markets characterised by rapid technological change and intense competition. They will have to have better communication skills, a penchant for collaboration, and a habit of life long learning.

In Japan 21.7 per cent of University students are in engineering. We in India, have about 7 per cent. It is scientifically proved that more the engineers, more is the economic growth. We have therefore to go a long way in this respect. Realising the demand many students are taking admission to engineering courses and their parents are also supporting, by paying higher fees in self-financed institutes, even by selling gold and other valuables. The peoples response to technical education is very commendable.

Multiple Approaches

Institutes of Technical education in India will have, however to provide a sound scientific base for the education of engineers. At present the facilities provided, by and large, are too inadequate, by world standards. In todays competitive world true that not one approach (MONOPOLY) through Government institutes is enough, but multiple approaches through the private initiative and imagination are badly needed. The task is too big for Government Institutes alone to cope with. The deficiency is too serious in scientific and technological skills, with the people in India and it is necessary to bridge the gap very fast without loosing any time. Merely producing graduates, with paper degrees is not wanted. World class standards are expected from private initiatives like in USA where private Universities are better, and more enterprising.

Education is an Economic Activity

Education has to be perceived now not only a social activity, as it used to be in the past, but also an economic activity. It is more so because it is intimately connected to industry, employment and income. Highly educated people get employment quickly, can start industry earn more income. Education system therefore will follow the laws of economics. A new class of Educational Entrepreneurs has therefore emerged, in India, as in abroad.

Privatisation in Technical Education is a trend not only in India, but the world over. It is so because it enables more productive utilisation of resources, for raising the scientific and technological capability of people. More importantly, privatisation is said to generate competition amongst Institutes and develops awareness amongst the students and people, which facilitates growth of technology at a faster rate in competitive world this is the need of the hour.

No single model of privatisation will suffice to cope with the challenges. Initiative from philanthropic organisations, industrial houses, teaching community, social and political agencies with collaborations internal and external are demanded. However, each one has limitations which need to be understood, it is for the worthy delegates in this convention to discuss debate and spell them out clearly.

It is true that today all is not will about privatisation. But all is not well in Governmentalisation either. There are advantages and disadvantages in both. There are situations where each one is suited most.

Government institutes have been all along paying the way, to be followed by others. There are higher costs of innovation, research, experimentation which can be incurred by Government and hence their role is significant, for all the time. This does not mean that private institutes do not and should not do innovation in fact innovation should be the character of all Institutes. Investment in innovation is in fact a highly paying proposition. No innovation - no progress more innovation - more progress.

Think Globally and Act Locally

It is a time when revolutionary changes are taking place in the world and so also in technical education. He is necessary to understand as to which way the global winds are blowing. What strategic changes others are making? It is for the distinguished delegates to take a global view and design a system fit for the nation.

It is said our institutes are teaching oriented and institutes in developed countries are research oriented. Indeed, we have to do introspection to find out whether it is possible to do good teaching over a career which spans 3-4 generations of new technology for one who is not engaged in research. This is to say that one cannot be a good teacher without constantly being engaged in research. This is yet another important aspect which invites serious consideration, and discussions in this convention.

It is essential for each institute more so in private to update itself and share vision of overall system of technical education and its goals, a concept expressed by the phrase - "Think globally and act locally".

There are technology parks, innovation centres, incubators attached to Higher Education Institutes in other countries. Professors, in Private Universities elsewhere like in U.S.A. have led the revolutionary changes in economy and industry. The famous Silicon Valley was a dream of two professors in the Stanford University which is private. With the persuasion of Prof. Terman the dream is realised. Similarly in several other countries like in Germany, Japan new opportunities, new avenues, new ideas for business trade and commerce are first thought of in Universities more so in private and then implemented on ground. Shall our institutes show wisdom, take initiative and play a crucial role in development?

Foreign Collaborations have Propelled Indian Industry and Earned Wealth

We see all around that many industries with huge investment are sick. Many industries are using obsolete technology. For modernisation they are going to foreign collaborators. Do we in academic institutes have to be silent spectators? or we have to go nearer to industry and win their confidence? Do we academicians have to show vision to provide the new technology to industry? Academicians in other countries are doing this. Institutes in Japan, USA and Germany earn their 1/3 budget from contract research.

They have technology transfer and patent offices. Do we have them? If not, we have to know where we are with respect to world, and decide where and how we want to go. Our institutes legitimate function is like heart to our body, which constantly purifies blood and pumps back in to all organs.

Innovation and Technology Transfer Wanted

This convention should discuss the organisational innovations necessary to promote pumping of new life and blood for doing Innovation and Technology Transfer. When institutes in private sector could do this in other countries, why we can't do in this country? Quality of educational institutes is not measured alone now by percentage of passing of students but by patents and Technologies generated. Their wealth is measured more in terms of Intellectual property. Are we any where near to this? We have a high potential and promise. If we have the will and skill it is possible to actually realise the potential. For want of innovativeness the nation is at risk and hence all have to hurry up.

As a Chairman of ISTE Maharashtra and Goa Section may I can for all engineering educators from both private and public institutes to work together nationally to improve the engineering education system. Foremost it should establish closer links connections amongst education, industry and research and develop a innovative character. This is the crying need of economy. In Germany, the professor in an University is also a director research in public sector research laboratory. He has two hats, one in University and the other in industry.

The Institutes should now discuss, new ideas, generate new technologies and make most regardless whether they are in private or public sector by adopting professionalism. Both are supporting to each other and essential for the nation, without privatisation in technical education the nation would have been at greater risk. This is well realised by even the one time opponents of privatisation. They must however evaluate their own performance constantly from the view point of all stake holders and in the context of national goals and visions.

9

An Overview of Engineering Education in India

Introduction

Science and technology is advancing today at a much faster rate than at any previous time. There has been a mushrooming of scientific findings in the last two decades, and new dimensions to professional and technician skills have become open. As a consequence demands made on engineering education have greatly changed. Rapid advances in science and technology have rendered the existing system insufficient for engineers and technicians both in respect of quality and quantity. As is economic, social and technological development to review the existing system and tailor it to suit the requirements of today and possibly those of tomorrow. In this article, it is attempted to explain the objectives of modern engineering education, and the ways to achieve them. .

Objectives of Engineering Education

Engineering profession has certain obligations to society. To continue to offer services in improving living and working conditions, devising ways and means to effect saving in efforts and materials, safety to society and so on. The forefronts of basic sciences are continually advancing and opening new areas for engineering endeavour. An engineer has to be alert and be able to assimilate and translate the advances of science in engineering practice. Thus, engineering is far from static and essentially a creative profession. Engineering education has therefore a goal to prepare men fully competent to do the professional practice independently and further raise the same to new heights through practice and research. It follows that education in college should produce engineers who can do the function of engineering analysis, design of construction, production, or operation. He should also be able to bring the designed project in reality. Further engineering education should inspire the student with necessary spirit, and enable him to deal with new situations with fundamental approach on his own initiative and confidence. He should develop a desire and sense for involvement and taking an active hand in changing things in the profession. Thus, the aims of engineering education lie much beyond training and employment. The new situations they have to handle in profession often involve social, economical, political and technical elements. Problems are seldom in well defined form. An engineer has to be able to sort out the problems, and simplify the same without loosing its essential nature. Further he should be able to think of a right approach to attack, evaluate and test the results at each stage.

Existing System and its Deficiencies

The existing system of engineering education in most of the colleges in our country seems to be an extension of the high school system, wherein it is contended that learning is proportional to attendance in class room. In engineering colleges 75 per cent attendance is compulsory. Many students attend classes out of this compulsion and consider classroom to be a place of entertainment instead of learning. Of the same class there are many divisions instruction being repeated for all the divisions in all the subjects as in high school. Curricula remain static for years. Teachers teach the subjects with a narrow outlook without any reference to the practice of the day. Teachers are isolated from professional practice and research and have no opportunity to be directly involved in them and remain in contact with the forefronts of the scientific developments in the subjects. A teacher who somehow keeps himself abreast though passively of the developments by reading journals and so on has no opportunity to deliver the advance material to students, because it is not included in the curriculum and obviously not asked for by external examiner. Students are more examination minded and have therefore no interest in listening to such things of advance knowledge.

In spite of the fact that several Indian Standard codes have been evolved and adopted, universities have not yet insisted on instruction in the use of these codes, which is a thing to be done every day by a practising engineer. The teacher is not many a times the examiner for his students. University believes more in external examiner. The teacher has therefore no opportunity to know the performance of his students in examination and adjust his teaching for the next batches.

Learning process aims at examination, wherein students have to memorise the subject-matter and reproduce the same mechanically in the paper. Learning is wrongly considered to be a passive process as if students absorb knowledge from what their teacher says. It has also become a narrow speciality of the subject. For example, learning to design plate and shell roofs. Students learn mathematical derivations and such other treatment to a very great extent, without adequate consideration to the methods of its construction, economic, and other feasibility aspects to bring the design in reality. It therefore does not take place as a liberal art for the profession. Students do not come to know the problems involved in the practical application, and are therefore labelled as theoritical engineers. They do not come up to the problems in profession while taking education and are obviously not prepared to meet them. One often hears too many complaints about the irrelevance of the offerings of the engineering courses. Obselete and outdated knowhow is taught at many places, and for current and advance knowledge there is no time for learning. It is therefore no wonder if products of our institutions cannot step in and stand independently in profession. Those who are supposed to create and provide jobs for others become themselves a burden to society. Best judged students of colleges desire to be hirelings, and the second grade men with forced circumstances form the code of employers and decision-makers. Engineers produced by our colleges are poor in practical respects and that they should take lessons from practising engineers. It is a common grievance of the people emerging out of colleges that all their education is a passive experience and they are not prepared to take active hand in changing things and bringing about a different social order.

Reforms Needed

The contention that learning is proportional to attendance does not hold good in case of higher education. Students seeking admission to engineering courses have brilliant career. Learning to them is largely a matter of stimulation and guidance, rather than tution. Today there is a grate deal of over instruction in the college and students are reluctant to attend all that. Regardless of how a teacher teaches every student learns at his own rate that too at has won initiative and efforts.

It would therefore be right to abandon the attendance system in classroom. Engineering students recognise the responsibility of preparing drawings and such other works themselves. The efore, insistence on doing the drawing within the four walls of the college should be given up. For better learning to take place they need more of freedom and less of supervision. They should have liberty to do it at home or in college. The number of theory lectures for each subject may be reduced allowing more of free time for self-learning. Thorough lectures they should receive a good introduction to each chapter of the subject and its full scope, alongwith the knowledge required for professional practice and latest developments. What is given in textbooks may be passingly referred, as students, have no interest in listening to them. They understand it better by reading the well written books themselves. A good academic freedom to students and staff is a practice in West Germany and many other developed countries. It is indeed the backbone of their so successful education system. They experience that academic freedom is very essential to develop creative thinking in the young and energetic minds. When students drive their studies themselves and by self initiative they are prepared best for getting actively involved in profession and attempting to raise the same to new heights, as is the primary objective of engineering education.

To enable teacher to deliver right type of material to students through lectures, he needs to have association with the professional practice and also research in the field. It is an observation that when a teacher divides his time equally in teaching research, and practice prepared to lecture in classroom. Being in contact with profession he experiences problems and after sorting them out-puts them to research in his faculty. He could also evaluate and test the outcome of research at each state and extend the same in practice. This knowledge gained from research, and supplemented with that from experiences flows automatically in classes and the young prospective engineers are greatly benefited by that. While passing out from college they come up to the forefronts of scientific developments in each subject. A synchronised relation and feedback system in teaching research, and practice is best possible in this way. A professor is then rightly able to serve as a source of academic impulses in the society. Engineering college should then justly become a seat of learning, and a leading unit in the process of economic and technological development. In developed countries this system prevails. Every institution engages itself in teaching and research. It is, therefore, the need of time that our engineering colleges do not limit themselves to merely teaching but apply themselves also in research, as is being done in foreign countries.

Most of the industries in our country are functioning in collaboration with companies in foreign countries. Development plans of these industries, howsoever minor they may be, are, implemented with the help of their counterparts. Today there is a potential of knowhow available, with laboratory equipment at engineering colleges, which can be gainfully utilised for such work. But because Government allows industry to run to their collaborators indiscriminately the knowhow at colleges remains idle and in turn education suffers. It would therefore be right to curtail foreign collaboration at least to the extent of development plans and divert the work to colleges. Participation of college staff should also be invited in the preparation of Government project designs. Today engineers of the departments such as B&C, I&P D, CPWD, etc. prepare the engineering designs of the projects, and also check the same. Because checking is done by the same department which prepares it, it has become just a formality, and mistakes are carried in execution. In fact, the purpose of checking designs is best served if it is done by a different agency. If checking of designs of Government projects is directed to college staff, they will be able to bring fresh view points in the design, and do it best in the light of latest developments in the subjects. This in turn assists the cause of education. Today students seeking admission to engineering colleges have little background of industry. Particularly those coming from rural areas whose number is large. They have absolutely no idea of the field in which they want to make career. In the absence of any practical training before admission they cannot decide interests in the branch of engineering, they choose. They find it difficult to corelate theory they learn with the practice. Introduction of practical training before admission and during vacations will enable the students to better appreciate the lectures. Teachers need not spend time and energy in describing elementary things. Workship practice in colleges may be altogether stopped. Six months practical training should be prescribed as precondition for admission. Training could be according to the branch of engineering, which would be naturally different for different branches. The idea of practical training is usually acceptable, but a difficulty is often put forward that the industry is not ready to accept the responsibility to train young prospective engineers. Industrialists do not want to suffer even slightest inconvenience in the cause of education and yet expect to have well educated and trained men from colleges. Government should therefore in national interest make it obligatory for industry to impart practical training to students, as it is obligatory to observe labour welfare.

The curriculum of courses should look more forward than behind. New subjects such as computer programming, advanced mathematics and so on should be introduced, Management Science is achieving importance in this technological age. Knowing only engineering design is not enough. In executing the design he has to deal with labour, salesmen, fellow men, etc. who bring to him new problems daily. An engineer should therefore learn modern scientific methods of projects planning and scheduling such as CPM/PERT, and more important to get well alongwith others. He must also learn public speaking, public relations, and psychology to give him confidence in his management duties. Syllabi of the subjects need not be spelled out in details as is the case today. They should be broad in nature giving just an outline of the subject. Details of curriculum may be left to teachers, who on having freedom may add or delete things as they deem fit from time to time and with reference to the practice of the day. Thus, curriculum will not remain static but change with time.

To bring students more in active participation in learning, group discussions, attending seminars and symposiums should be encouraged. Curriculum should include project report writing and a dissertation. Dissertation should be a sole creation of the student and done preferably after all his theory papers are over. He should find a problem for himself, work on that and draw out conclusions. Students derive great pleasure from their original creation, and they should be permitted to do so. Memory oriented examinations will have to be stopped. Questions set should be aimed at testing the candidates intelligence and critical faculty and not merely his capacity to memorise facts and figures, special seminars and orientation courses if necessary should be organised to train examiners for this purpose.

ENGINEERING EDUCATION IN CRISIS

In a liberalised economy a phenomenon is observed that Universities from countries like Australia, USA and UK have taken out an aggressive drive to market education world over, including India. They have opened technology transfer and marketing departments, as companies have, to make sale of education. They are advertising frequently in newspapers and holding meetings with students, parents and management of colleges in India. They are opening learning centres and giving affiliation to private colleges. These outside universities which have proven experience, reputation and credibility with employers, especially multinational corporations, are more likely to attract the best of our students. To a great extent, in globalisation and liberalisation, if we do not upgrade our institutions they are likely to capture our better students, and our colleges may be left with mediocres. Our Universities may then become like Zilla Parishad or municipality schools. Thus, there is an external pressure on our higher education system to improve and compete globally.

To compare the situation with industry, it is observed that multinational companies in liberalised economy have been, since long coming to India and posing threat to Indian companies. It is also resulting in technology transfer, collaboration and improvement in our companies in respect of products and processes. This is viewed as a welcome development for it is beneficial to consumers although putting pressure on producers to manufacture goods on international standards at competitive prices.

A somewhat similar situation has arisen now in higher education. Our Univesities and especially engineering education institutes which are crucial to national economy have to face competition. Will they welcome this competition from foreign counterparts? The need to understand the methodology of functioning of Universities in foreign countries and emulate. The students and employers who are customers are presently very dissatisfied with the present approaches of the Universities and colleges which are not teaching what is wanted and also not assuming the legitimate role of providing technology to Industry.

If we look at Universities in countries like Germany, USA, Japan there is a striking difference in respect of research. These Universities offer flexible courses permitting students to learn what they like, giving access to students in national-level research projects. Besides, the professors, for example, in Germany have two hats, one in University and another in National Research Laboratory. Similarly, the senior research scientists in research laboratories have on reciprocal basis Chairs in Universities. This kind of integration of University with research laboratory is said to be a great strength in taking the country technologically forward. It is a missing link in our country.

Their Universities have also marketing and technology transfer departments which play a key role in regional development. They have their own technology parks and University companies to give technology push to economy and escort students for jobs in industry. The proportion of students studying engineering is much large: 15 to 20 per cent of the total student population as against only 7 per cent in our country. Universities generate 33 per cent of their income through research contracts and patent sale. These missions and visions are conspicuously absent in our Universities.

The present Universities in our country on the other hand, have very little interaction with industry and regional development authorities. Industry has no confidence in research capability of Universities. The vital element of innovation is missing from higher education. The relationship between the university and Industry truly has to be complementary to each other. Industry and institutes be interdependent and revitalising each other. But the actual situation is far from desirable. The leaders in education and leaders in Industry alongwith government ought to react strategically taking into account the policies and practices elsewhere in the world and restore the desirable relationship.

When food problem in India was acute in 50s and 60s it was predicted by the World Bank that people would die in 70s and 80s out of hunger. Thanks to the strategic and unique measures taken by the then Government like establishment of separate agricultural Universities to do research, education and extension in an integrated manner. The agricultural Universities are not only educating students but they are also developing new varieties of seeds and scientific practices and carrying them to farmers. Without this, the agriculture in India would have remained primitive and the food problem would have become more acute and people starved.

Similar situation has arisen now in the industrial production and productivity which is far too low by world standards. We are importing technologies more and more from abroad and yet the industry is becoming sick it is obvious for how long can we remain competitive on borrowed knowledge? We have to learn to do research in Universities and provide access to young students to do research. Without this the higher education is less likely to improve and the workforce for industry and economy may remain less competent despite the potential. It is high time that we go for technical Universities integrating the three, namely, education, research and extension like in Germany and Japan. This is also recommended by UNESCO in one of its reports especially for developing countries. It is further emphasised in the report that the 5 year plans of national development and universities should have closer co-operation with the Universities.

Today, the Universities in India are doing only policing trying to prevent copying in examinations. They have become only controller of examinations rather than the seats of research and learning. Autonomous status to University depertments and colleges is prescribed by the new national policy on education 1986 but till today not much progress in this field has taken place. It is mainly because or leaders in education both in colleges and Universities are lacking knowledge and confidence in this new system. Unfortunately, they are not with the world in this respect. The coming of foreign Universities in India will give them an opportunity to see from closer distance their strategies and management styles and it is hoped that this should induce good effects in our system.

To conclude, coming of foreign Universities in India is a boon for students in higher education and a golden chance for institutes to learn better policies and practices. We hope that our Universities will welcome them and associate closely. A major overhaul is needed in higher education, especially technical, to make it globally competitive. It is hoped the Government and industry will take bold steps to set up Technical Universities like agricultural Universities to integrate research, education and extension. It may certainly cost, but the cost of not doing are prohibitively high.

Prof. Michaer Porter in his book "The Competitive Advantage of Nations" based on studies in ten developed countries wrote that countries are industrially advanced which have emphasised engineering education. Secondly, those nations which have more of Technical Universities are more advanced. Thirdly, the model of Technical University is more productive and effective for technical education than a comprehensive university.

Fourthly, the nations where universities and CSIR like laboratories remain in network, share research facilities and findings provide access to research to young students are more advanced.

PERFORMANCE PLANNING AND APPRAISAL WHY AND HOW?

Set-goals-then Measure and Meet Them

One important role of a technical institute is to impart education to the students to enable them to acquire uptodate knowledge of their fields, so that they become an asset for the socioeconomic development of the nation. In the present situation many new technologies are emerging. The rate of change of technology is so fast that an individual faculty member or institute can easily suffer from obsolescence if it is not sensitive enough to all these changes and don't adopt ways for coping with change at both individual and institutional levels. All this requires an effective method of performance planning for individual faculty. The first step in performance appraisal is to define the job, various duties and various expected goals for individuals as well as for institution and the criterion on which performance will be judged. The various primary functions of a faculty member are -

(i) *Institutional activities:* These include scheduled teaching in classroom and laboratory, development of teaching materials and methods, student advising and counselling, conducting examination and correcting papers, etc.

(ii) *Academic research:* This includes the supervision at Bachelor, Master and Doctoral levels, carrying out research work and publishing the work in journals. This alone enable teacher to teach relevant to the needs, else he tends to teach irrelevant.

(iii) *Consultancy:* To take the live problems from industries and work on it, and transfer technology to industry.

(iv) *Sudents activities:* To take part in various extra curricular activities, to guide the students for their future plan, various opportunities, etc.

(v) Continuing Engineering Education.

The University grants commission strongly urges for good performance by teachers because teacher performance is linked with the task of maintaining and co-ordinating standards. The various factors which influence the quality of education and its contribution to the national development are the quality, competence and character of teachers. The various problems which will affect the performance of teachers are -

- Self-competence.
- Attitude towards the work.
- Sensitivity to change in environment.
- Delegation of authority.
- Lack of clear definition of his role in the total educational system.
- Performance appraisal system.
- While doing the planning for teachers the following points should be taken into consideration.
- It should be specific, clearly mentioning the various activities of the teacher.
- As far as possible the objectives should be measurable in some way.
- Every objective should have a time limit on it.
- The objective should not be beyond the capability.
- Plan should be challenging so that they get a job satisfaction.
- To ensure good performance the existence of an effective performance appraisal system is a must.

Performance Appraisal of a Teacher

Performance appraisal makes the teacher accountable for his work. To carry out the performance appraisal of a teacher, it is necessary that teacher should know what is expected of him, how much is expected of him and what happens if he does better or bad. An effective performance appraisal system for faculty is vital for optimising the contribution of individual faculty member to the institutional performance. The NPE has recognised the need of formulating the performance appraisal system for teachers which should be open, participative and data based. The AICTE will evolve feasible staff appraisal system and corresponding norms, through extensive consultation with state government, Director of Technical Education Institutions, professional bodies and teachers representatives.

(a) ***Existing System and its Deficiencies***

The present scenario of faculty appraisal in technical institutions, although widely varying, have deficiencies which are in brief as under:

The present system of performance appraisal is a most unscientific system. It consists of preparing confidential reports annually by the head of the Departments.

The report appraises the person rather than the work done by him. In the recent days a recent days a self-assessment form is to be filled up by the teacher, which is again reviewed by the Head of the Department. The confidential report gives vague and ambiguous terms. One cannot interpret the meaning from these statements. The reports are the opinion about the individual. This can be taken as a personal criticism. There is no communication of the appraisal to the teacher at most of the places. If adverse communication is made the teachers are found to revolt, and reply back. Another demerit of this type of appraisal is that the lack of scholastic authenticity on the part of the appraiser. As teachers in technical institutions belong to a wide spectrum of disciplines, no single supervisor has the academic competence to evaluate all of them.

(b) ***Proposed Performance Appraisal System for Engineering College Teacher***

As the performance appraisal is a system of controlling the work, not the people, due care should be taken while formulating it. The performance appraisal involves the institution, department and individual faculty member. As the performance appraisal system is a powerful mechanism for translating overall institutional goals to individual faculty member, it should be open, participative, data based.

Teachers are always apprehensive about the manner in which the performance appraisal is done. In USA, when a merit pay scheme was offered to the teachers by president Regan in

1983, teachers' organisation like the American Federation of Teachers (AFT) rejected it mainly because of the fear that an uncertain and unreliable standard might be adopted in evaluating teacher. Thus, it is felt that teacher should be involved in the performance appraisal system so that they are more likely to consider the appraisal and the system as fair. They also get the knowledge of what is expected of them, from having opportunities to discuss problems and get confirmation that they are doing things well. Thus, the various deficiencies in existing system of appraisal like appraising the person rather than work, can be removed if the appraisal is open and participative.

Fig. 9.1 Shows the proposed model of performance appraisal for teachers

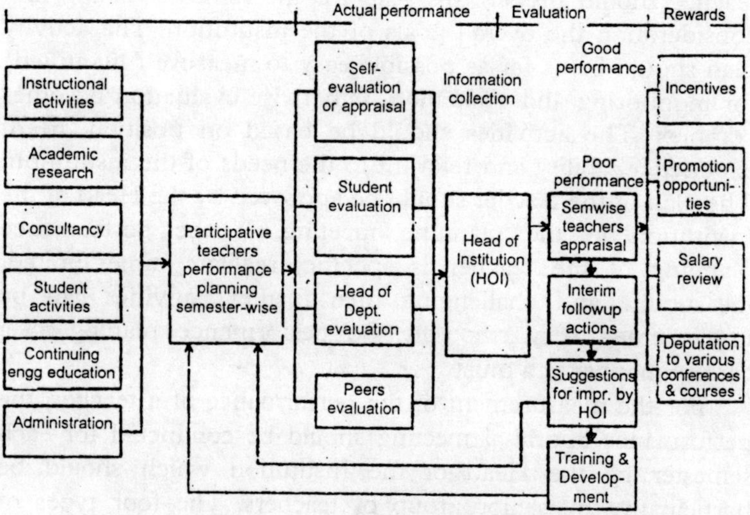

Fig. 9.1 : Block diagram representation of proposed model for Perfomance appraisal of teacher.

The performance appraisal system should be data based. If data available for evaluation is inadequate it is very difficult to take decision for giving rewards, promotions, etc. the data available for evaluation should be reliable one. The data collected may be unreliable if there is existence of rivalry between groups, inadequate attention to issues related to interpersonal relationship etc. Hence, it is very essential to collect the information regarding the teachers performance from a number of reliable sources. In the model as shown in Fig.9.1, the data can be collected by the Head of the Institution from students, peers and Head of the Department. Thus, the proposed model consists of four types of evaluation of teachers performance: (i) students evaluation, (ii) Self-apprasial, (iii) Peers evaluation, (iv) Head of Department/Supervisor evaluation.

Before evaluating the teachers' performance, preparation of a suitable work plan for each teacher is very important activity is the whole process of performance planning and appraisal. The Principal and all Heads of the Departments should conduct a meeting of teachers in each semester to prepare the work plan of each teacher. Before planning meeting, each teacher should prepare his plan for the semester taking into consideration the overall goals of the institution. The activity plan should be as far as possible easy to measure (quantified) for monitoring and evaluation. Otherwise evaluation becomes complex. The activities should be based on position, need, experience, ability and relevant to the needs of the institution. The plan of the teacher should be approved by the Head of the Institution in the planning meeting. If the performance planning of the teacher is specific, realistic, time limited, measurable and challenging then further activities can be implemented very smoothly. So performance planing in a careful manner is a must.

For the measurement of the performance of a teacher, the performance appraisal meeting should be conducted for each semester by the Head of the Institution which should be participative by senior group of teachers. The four types of evaluation already mentioned should be taken into consideration for studying the poor performance and good performer. For each type of evaluation, a detailed questionnaire can be prepared and filled in by student, self, supervisor and peers. In student evaluation the students should be selected from each group like academically very good, average, good in extra-curricular activity etc. the questionnaire for student evaluation should have questions on teachers as follows:

- Preparation of the subject.
- Presentation of the subject.
- Personality, character, punctuality.
- Readiness to help the students.
- Classroom management, use of various modern teaching aids.
- Behaviour with students, participation in student activities, both extra-curricular and co-curricular activities.

For each question, some credit should be given. For each type of evaluation percentage given should be fixed. Similar questionnaire can be prepared for other types of evaluation also. Then total percentage obtained by the teacher should be used to decide the performance of the teacher.

If the teacher gets above 75 per cent then he should be given grade "Excellent", for 60 to75 per cent "Best", for 50 to 60 per cent, "Good" and for below 50 per cent "Poor". If the teacher gets excellent and best grades for consecutively three years he should be given increments, promotion, etc. If the teacher gets poor grade for successively there years then he should be given punishment accordingly. For improving the performance of poor teacher. Head of the institution should conduct interim follow-up meetings. In the meeting, the teacher should give the reasons for his poor performance. After hearing the causes of poor

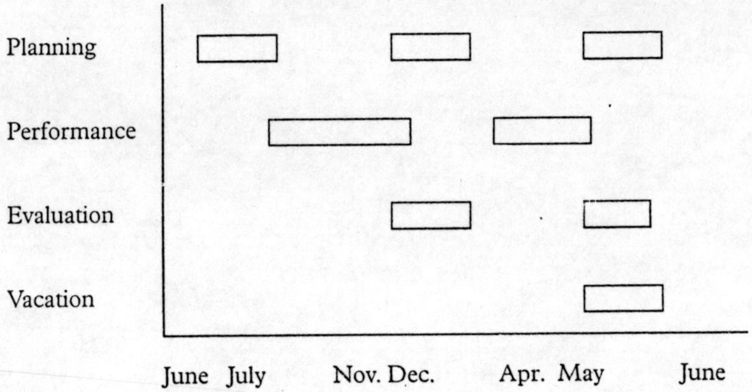

Fig. 9.2: Performance Planning and Appraisal Cycle.

performance he will suggest the way for improving the performance and if needed he may be deputed to training and development courses.

Fig. 9.2 shows the Bar Chart of performance planning and appraisal cycle for one academic year. Normally for any institution first term period is July - November and second term period is December - April. For each semester, planning and evaluation should be made. In the month of June - July planning of teacher/institution should be done and then between July to November teachers have to work according to their planning. Then in the participative appraisal meeting for the first semester (i.e. in November - December) the evaluation of the teacher and replanning for the next semester can be made. The Bar Chart also shows these activities for the second semester.

10

Technical Education in Private Sector

Too Low Investment in Education by Government has Failed the Nation

People demand on technical education in terms of quality and quantity, in India, is grossly unmet. Priority allocated by a family in its home budget for education in general, technical in particular, is much high, higher than for building a house, buying a refrigerator, T.V., etc. People of low income group are seen spending their lifetime saving on technical education of their Children.

This Priority is, however, not reflected in Governments National/State budget. During first five year plan, we were spending 7.86 per cent of GNP on education. Till sixth five year plan, it consistently came down to 2.7 per cent of GNP, although now again picked up to 3.55 per cent.

Public investment on education in India is one of the lowest. It is, therefore, no wonder if per capita income is also one of the lowest. (U.S.$ 360). The nation has failed on account of this and all the problems like poverty, unemployment, communalism, blind faith, population growth, etc. have assumed high proportion.

Vast majority of education spending in all the nations is Govt. financed and they devote far fewer private resources to education. For example, in U.S., 7.4 per cent of GNP (1977) is allocated to education, out of which 6.3 per cent of GNP in public spending and only 1.1 per cent of GNP is private.

The education commission 1964 - 66, and New Education Policy, 1986 recommended public investment of 6 per cent of

GNP but it has not been cared for by planners. Asian tiger countries Taiwan, Hong Kong, Malaysia have been spending on education as high as 11 per cent of GNP and they attribute credit for their progress to this strategy of high investment on education. The world average investment on education is 5.6 per cent of GNP (1978) almost two times more than investment in India.

It is this deficiency in education budget on the part of Government, which has led to spur in privatisation and followed by commercialisation of education, first for nursery then primary, secondary and now for higher education.

Now the Supreme Court in its recent judgment has declared that, right to education is a fundamental right, even in the sphere of Higher Education and laid down the principle that "admission should be on merit, rather than capacity to afford".

The underlying principle being that of equal opportunity to all, which is followed in all developed and developing countries. If education opportunities are unequally distributed, because of inequalities in the distribution of income, and hence the capacity of individuals to finance investment in education, then it will perpetuate inequalities of income in future, since earning power is related to workers education.

Privatisation has a inherent tendency to bypass legal and constitutional social provisions like reservations, and equity. This would have to be guarded through a deliberate, conscious effort and avoided. They should not become a cause of segregation of society but bring about integration, which is restored by supreme court decision by prescribing 50 per cent free seats and 50 per cent paying seats in unaided college.

Privatisation should not Result into Commercialisation

Privatisation in education is not new to this country. Schools and colleges were started by Tilak, Maharshi Karve, Madan Mohan Malviya, Karmaveer Bhaurao Patil. But what is new is commercialisation of education, and profit making (unofficial).

The education entrepreneurs of today are not motivated by philanthropic considerations like in past, but by motives of name, fame and profit. In U.S.A. and other countries they have resorted to only mild privatisation and not total, like ours collecting 100 per cent cost from students. Resources are mobilised for the cause of education besides fees from students (50 per cent) from private sources, namely the industry, (20 per cent) and 19 per cent from Government, 11 per cent from donations. The tuition fees have gone up substantially, but yet they do not meet up the full cost of education. Universities and schools undertake research projects from industry on payment, to provide financial support to technical education. Ram Murthi Commission (1990) has also recommended differential fee system, and said that only 75 per cent of cost of education to be collected from students.

This is a new world, according to W.W. Rostow, full of opportunities in hi-tech, to earn, for those who have its knowledge and skills. Realising this, people are rushing to learn new technology. Education is being viewed not as a social service but an economic activity. Government institutions, inherently, are slow to respond to peoples needs and hence privatisation.

Forms of Privatisation

Privatisation assumes various forms:

(a) When the institute is founded managed and maintained by Government it is zero privatisation.
(b) When aided by Government, (100 per cent) managed and maintained by a society appointed by Government, it is mild privatisation.
(c) When aided by Government up to 90 per cent, managed and maintained by private society, it is termed intensive privatisation.
(d) When unaided by Government managed and maintained by private society, it is termed as total privatisation.

All forms of organisations are obliged to comply with the statutory provisions.

There is a world wide revolution in thinking, perception and vision in technical education. New forms of innovative organisations to capture market opportunities in education are taking birth. Equality in opportunity to the most down and out people is also being kept in view, in all countries, especially in developing. Provision of scholarship and loans to poor and deserving students are on increasing scale. Japan is reported to be giving more loans (refundable), while European countries give scholarship (non-refundable). We in India give both, loans and scholarship, but the quantum is too small, in particular that of loans.

Professionalism and Accreditation is the Need of the Hour

More importantly, the professionalism and Accreditation in education, teaching, researching is becoming the order of the day. Innovations in curricula, teaching methods, transfer of technology, are gaining value to make learning most effective, purposeful and yet reducing the cost, time and effort. This demands professionalism on the part of teachers, and management in colleges, otherwise they would get reduced to commercial teaching shops, teaching old, outdated and irrelevant things.

The paper lays stress on these two aspects namely -

(i) Professionalism; adherence to norms and standards prepared by AICTE and university for colleges, and

(ii) Their accreditation by independent body, evaluating their rating and worth for performing the legitimate responsibilities. Establishment of accreditation board by AICTE, is in process. It is this aspect which is vitally linked to success of privatisation. In the absence of accreditation, it is not possible to make distinction in the standard of education of various colleges. Neither the management nor the students know where they are and where they tend to go.

The Balance Sheet

The balance sheet of unaided private engineering colleges and polytechnics is presented below:

Undesirable Aspects

1. Some institutes are reported to be financially exploiting the students, parents and the society (unofficially). Now, with the decision of supreme court, it is hoped that it will be curbed.

2. Many institutions do not provide proper education, due to lack of laboratory facilities, trained teachers and laboratory staff.
3. Some institutes do not pay wages properly to the employees.
4. The discipline in colleges, law and order in cities or towns where the institutes are located has deteriorated, because of influx of students from outside state and lack of management capability to cope with.
5. The discipline in universities is adversely affected.
6. Some managements are unofficially siphoning out money for selfish and election purposes.
7. These colleges are a cause of segregation of students, rich and poor, which according to a proven theory perpetuates the gap, and so it is a constitutional objection.
8. The management is found lacking vision and professionalism.
9. Intentions of some managements are doubtful.
10. Some are exploiting the weakness of Government.
11. Due to lack of professionalism it is observed that colleges are deficient in teaching staff, laboratory equipment and other facilities. Teachers from such institutes now dominate the board of studies and other academic activities in University. Rules of passing have been made easy, term work marks are given much more, than they deserve, as a result a student who just passes in theory gets first class. Question papers set in examination are easy, and full of mistakes. Norms and standards prescribed for higher education are not followed. The number of lectures delivered actually are only half of prescribed. Professional approach is expected to control all above and turn out competent engineers.

Desirable Aspects

1. They are meeting the peoples demand on technical education, at least of those who can afford.

2. Some colleges/polytechnics which are located in rural areas, have taken Hi-Tech to rural area for which they deserve to be complemented and rewarded.
3. In rural areas, they have set up colleges where Government would not have set up even technical schools. Their contribution in rural development is noteworthy.
4. They have been producing engineers and meeting skill shortages of industry.
5. Many jobs are generated in these colleges on sustained basis for example lecturers, lab-assistants, clerks, peons, and on temporary basis like in construction of buildings manufacture furniture, equipment, etc.
6. The development of colleges have been very fast as compared to similar institutes in Government.
7. These colleges have created a base for technology development and are useful in closing the technology gap.
8. Many managements have certainly shown an enterprising spirit. They are highly motivated for giving service to society.
9. Lot of financial resources have been mobilised within the state for the cause of education. So also substantial capital has come from outside state.

The institutes are a social asset under Society Act, and not a personal property. Society has therefore become richer.

Suggestions

1. Appoint a University nominee on the management of each college. Funds collected ought to be used only for institute. This should be ensured.
2. Government should take a lead in training teachers. The present standard of education is very poor, for want of trained teachers. The state is a beneficiary of the graduates coming out from such institutes, and hence it must assume at least the responsibility of training teachers.
3. Start postgraduate, Ph.D. programmes in Government/aided colleges, in vacations where teachers from

private colleges can continue further study. Developing high level technical manpower is the crying need of these colleges. Without this, quality of education will deteriorate.

4. Government should establish technical Universities forthwith, one in each of the four regions to properly regulate admission teaching exam. etc. One of the existing Government colleges could be elevate to university status for quickness in shaping the private colleges.
5. Antecedents of the students coming from outside state should be duly verified, so that they do not create trouble for colleges and cities. The colleges should attempt to attract only Scholars from other states and not gundas.
6. Government should Grant financial aid and loans to students who are financially poor. Government should provide financial grants/loan to all colleges. State gains a lot from these institutes, and so it should share the expenditure also.
7. The colleges should be allowed to go global to earn foreign exchange. This is a time when market boundaries are rapidly shifting and demands for globalisation and innovation are becoming a rule. When India Government has taken the export drive, it should also export technical education, which more importantly provides a base for export of goods. Only quality education can be exported, and so they would have to improve the standards to international levels. It is an opportunity for Maharashtra to specialise in technical education, for which 'Quality' and 'Professionalism' are the key words.
8. "Accreditation" should be introduced by Government or a statutory body forthwith, so that the students parents, and society know the rating of colleges.
9. Aided colleges need to be granted academic autonomy and Government colleges be converted into autonomous or deemed Universities. Government

ought to make them more open through organisational model to permit them to offer flexible responses to market needs, private colleges emulate them and hence this is necessary.

10. Learning from the experience of other countries in the world, it may be submitted for consideration that the technical education ought to be delinked from education Ministry and linked to Industry Ministry, without which it is difficult to make technical education and research relevant and useful.

Innovative Private Initiative Needed

The concept of privatisation of education is practiced in USA and several other countries. In fact, the best Universities of USA are private, for ex. M.I.T. Boston. In Maharashtra, private initiative ought to be viewed as supplementary to government effort. The number of engineers, in India today for the huge size of country, abundant raw materials, and huge population are goo few, only one tenth of what we ought to have. India cannot hope to utilise the natural resources optimally and raise the standard of living of the vast masses, with so few engineers. In another five years, if India wants to catch up with the world the number of colleges would have to again double, despite the unemployment of engineers. Engineering career will remain in higher demand in years to come. There are 2,90,000 engineering students in small country like Germany while India has only 68,000. Small country like Malaysia, Singapore, Taiwan, etc. have far more engineering students than India.

Technical education is very crucial to industrial competitiveness. Percentage share of Maharashtra in national industrial production is found to be consistently going down from 60 per cent to 40 per cent. This has to be a cause of concern while shaping technical education in the state.

(a) India share in world trade has gone down from 2.25 per cent in 1950 to 0.54 per cent in 1992 (news item in financial express on 12th December, 1992).

(b) Incremental Capital Output Ratio (ICOR) of India is very high, 6.11. Highest in Asian region as against 3.33

of Malaysia, 3.37 of Korea, 4.82 of Singapore. It means we are investing more and getting less, which is due largely to shortage of technological inputs.

(c) The output per employee in Indian industry is very low $1277, as against $ 20016 in Singapore and $ 67246 in Japan.

Building of a nation needs not only more engineers, but engineers with excellence and innovative ability. There is a whole renovation taking place in the world and we ought to have a look at that while making the decision. COMETT, technology parks, Entrepreneurship centres, Incubators, University Enterprise Training Partnership, etc. are developed and attached to almost every higher education institute elsewhere in the world. It is this development which has propelled the industry and economy of those nations. Our institutes would have to do that for which private initiative may be effective.

11

Financing of Technical Education

Is Expenditure on Education Non-productive?

Decades ago production and productivity depended only on hard work, sincerity and muscle power. This is no longer true. With rapid advances in Science and Technology, the older means of production have become uneconomical. The newer methods and machines require high technological and intellectual capabilities. Without education, more so technical education, increases in production with high productivity, reliability and cost effectiveness cannot be dreamed. For best utilisation of our available material and financial resources, it is necessary to have a competent human force, often it is said that there is no inadequacy of resources, but there is only inadequacy of their effective management. To quote PETER DRUCKER, under-developed countries are not underdeveloped; they are under managed.

Is Life Long Education Worth the Effort?

Education is required not only for obtaining a job, but also to retain it. For many jobs, their contents are changing very fast. A machine operator, for example, is now required to operate automatic, CNC Machines, which he can't do unless he learns again. Periodic retraining and experience-based learning can be represented as below:

(a) As a person works on his job, he learns and his competency increases, say at a rate α.

(b) As a person undergoes re-training, considerable knowledge output is given to him, and on his return from such training his competency increases at the rate $(\alpha + \Delta_1)$.

(c) As and when he is re-trained periodically, his competency would increase as $\alpha + \Delta_1 + \Delta_2 + ...$ each Δ representing additional level or rate of competency increase.

(d) Without continuous education and training his competency would increase only slowly and sometimes would decrease.

Findings of World Bank Study

A study conducted by World Bank has reported that Education in developing countries is not unproductive, but is actually highly productive. The rate of return from such investment (R.O.R.) on Educational Projects is about 100 per cent which no Industrial nor Agricultural Projects can ever match.

This fact, is very well recognised and further utilised in Zero Based Budgeting.

Zero Based Budgeting in Education

In conventional budgeting, financial provisions are made based on budgets and expenditure of previous years. The ongoing programmes, schemes and projects get priority. Many costs are just incurred because they have been budgeted for years. No fresh justification is necessary to obtain their sanction. Due to this approach, most of the financial resources given to an institution gets exhausted and little is left for new projects - the latter, although, are more feasible and are likely to be more worth-while than the older or ongoing schemes. In Zero Based Budgeting all the activities including the older and newer schemes, positions and cost centres are considered afresh. They are made to compete simultaneously, for the available financial resources. In U.S.A., this system is in operation for several years (in fact from 1960) and there are instances of many ongoing projects having been abandoned, in favour of new schemes. In a dynamic socio-economic situation it becomes desirable to reverse poor viable decisions rather than adhering to them.

To illustrate this point, let us consider budgeting of resources for programmes in B.A./M.A. in History, Geography, Political Sciences, or B.Sc./M.Sc. in Physics, Chemistry or B.E./M.E. in Engineering and Technology.

Budget provisions are being made for continuing Arts and Science Courses, though they are not much in demand. On the other hand, Engineering courses, although in great demand are not provided the necessary inputs. There are several Colleges where Arts Courses are offered, without many students in them just for the sake of continuation. Besides, teacher's salaries, valuable building space and other overhead expenses are poorly utilised.

Zero based Budgeting will question such situations and will bring out the cost effectiveness of such projects. It gives an early warning to the funding authorities that, in the light of emerging, continuously changing situations, it is no more useful to provide funds for infeasible/less-feasible ongoing programmes. It is also essential to explore ways and means to convert the existing programmes suitably by the necessary inputs to make them more relevant to the demands of students.

These require judicious and at times, hard decisions and these decisions are also difficult to implement due to a variety of factors. Conversion of the services of Staff for instance, poses a serious problem. However, retraining persons in areas or specialisations of their interest is feasible, this may be a solution. Retraining is good for individuals as well as for organisations, since they get trained personnel.

Zero Based Budgeting in Technical Institutions

Let us now take an Institutional situation of an Engineering College offering courses in only conventional branches of engineering such as Civil, Mechnical and Electrical engineering. These Colleges, with a little modification and some training to their teachers can switch over to more popular disciplines like Electronics, Computer engineering, etc. and similar programmes. Conventional budgeting will not detect this and will not indicate, well in time, that such alternatives are more worthwhile. The Zero Budgeting system facilities introspection of strengths and exploration of opportunities by its very inherent characteristic of fresh evaluation.

In Zero Based Budgeting, before an item is included in the budget, it is considered that the College on the Department is at Zero point, that is its assets are liquid and can be moulded as required. Considering the proposed activities of the year a list of the requirements is prepared without consideration of the availability or non-availability of the resources required. On this, the picture of what is available is superimposed and deviations and requirements are detected. It the available space is short of requirements it may have to be constructed, or altered by conversion. If old equipment is not needed, it is advisable to dispose it off and purchase new equipment instead of spending money to maintain and operate it. Thus, the system is dynamic in nature and responsive to fresh priorities.

For Technical Institutions, while it is true that adequate budget provision is not usually made, it is also true that whatever is provided is not utilised optimally. A sizable saving is possible by avoiding waste and worthwhile new activities can be conducted. For each of the activity requiring such positions, equipment, space, and any other resource, questions can be asked such as, can the activity be performed in a variety of ways? What are they? Which of them is better and cheaper? Thus, the Zero Based Budgeting gives a jolt against inertia to maintain *status quo*. It forces an organisation to move forward and remain competitive at every point of time. Inefficiency in cost planning and control is also detected well in time. Organisation capability to adopt to changes and to seize upon opportunities increases.

Zero Based Budgeting for Curricular Modernisation

Zero Based Budgeting is also applicable for the design of Courses and for curriculum development. For example, at the first or second year of engineering level subjects like Workshop Practice. Engineering Drawing, Surveying are being taught even today to students in Electronics Engineering taking away a lot of their time, while for introducing newer subjects like Computer Technology, Microprocessor Applications, CNC Machines, etc.

no time allotted to the curriculum. Thus, there is a need to prioritising the older and newer subjects, the solution becomes obvious. Zero Based Budgeting system, in principle, when used will thus lead to modernisation of syllabi, and the psychological tendency of man to cling to the past and to resist change is reduced. In the process of modernisation of curriculum some positions of teachers may become redundant. They have to be skilfully retrained to adopt to newer subjects. A continuous modernisation of Courses, diversification of specialisations of teachers, proper utilisation of space and equipment will lead to avoidance of obsolescence.

Other Aspects of Zero Based Budgeting

Newer methods of learning and teaching like "Distance Learning" through T.V. Network and use of Video films, are being developed in recent time. In subjects like Electronics, Instrumentation, Computer Engineering teachers of the required qualifications are not available in the required numbers. The new or alternative methods of teaching through video films can compete with conventional classroom teaching with implication on the budget for salaries of teachers. It may be desirable to divert funds for establishment for newer methods of teaching and learning and correspondingly reduce allocation on salaries of teachers.

Similarly, innovation in the examination systems and procedures are on the anvil. A lot of money is spent on the printing of question papers and in the conduct of examinations in the conventional manner. Besides expenditure of money, time and effort is also wasted. Zero Based Budgeting can be expected to question this system and bring about a change. Zero Based Budgeting also helps the authorities to achieve cost control and enable effective utilisation of resources allotted to various projects.

However, it is a technique, a tool in the hands of officers who matter most. It is not going to act by itself. It has to be used, and only when used in the proper spirit, it can provide benefits to the user.

CHALLENGES IN TECHNICAL EDUCATION WHERE ARE WE IN TECHNICAL LITERACY GLOBALLY?

It is being increasingly realised that wealth of a nation, depends not much on the material resources like land, water, minerals, etc. but more on the capability of the human resource especially in Scientific and Technological fields. Human Resources Development in todays dynamic economy, fast changing technology and competitive world has therefore assumed paramount importance. It is necessary not only for economic development but also for the social, political, spiritual and cultural growth of society, enabling the men and women to live worthy human being. Without the knowledge of Science and Technology our vast masses especially in rural areas would not be in a position to make optimal utilisation of the abundant natural resources. Technical education for people has become essential to make them self-reliant and to enable them to face bravely and resourcefully the challenges, ahead of them in 21st Century.

Technical Education for Human Resource Development of youths, middle aged, disadvantaged, professional and vocational personnel has a special role to play. Technically trained persons are a source of strength for national scientific industrial development.

Countries in the world have developed which have resorted to industrialisation. Rightly so, the Central Government and the State Governments in Five Year Plan have been laying high emphasis on industrialisation. However, industrialisation depends not so much on the natural resources, minerals, markets, but more on the technological capability of the people, which in turn depends on the quality of technical education acquired by them.

Technical education in India, till recently was aiming at development of skills oriented to the running and maintenance of industries. But presently, they have to aim at design and development of the newer models suiting to the local conditions at competitive price. The productivity of the various vocations and professions in the state, by and large, for their survival and growth needs to be stepped up to international standards. It has been low largely because of the poor content of the Science and Technology.

The role of Universities, Engineering Colleges, Polytechnics and other Technical Institutions in the present time are envisaged to be much different than the roles, they have performed earlier. They have to function as the rural areas, and disseminate the same to various walks of life by undertaking extension programmes of formal and non-formal education. As is heart to our body, so are they to the society. The capacity utilisation of established institutes has to be stepped up and facilities in newer areas would have to be introduced.

The paper aims at raising the pertinent issues, identifying challenges, and the peoples problems in technical education.

Challenges in Technical Education

(a) The challenges are imparting technical education on mass scale to the people, youths and adults is the first and foremost challenge. But for this the productivity of vast masses working in various vocations and professors in spite of their hard work, enthusiasm and sincerity is too low. The utilisation of resources like land, minerals, water, etc. is suboptimal. The utilisation of material and human resource in capital formation stage of projects and subsequently their capacity utilisation is far too low, hence this challenge.

(b) Improving quality/standard and relevance of education to meet the needs of working life, taking into account the emerging technologies, intellectual capabilities of people, and growing industrial needs, is the second challenge. It is necessary to create a work force of human resources capable enough to design, instal and maintain industries, competitive by nothing less than international standards. This is because of the recent trend of internationalism in trade and commerce. To fight with smuggling of goods from foreign countries in a right way, it is necessary to make our industrial products sophisticated in terms of quality, reliability, finish and yet cost effective. This, of course, demands technical education of better quality to our masses.

(c) Forecasting the pattern of establishment of industries and employment in future and shaping the technical education in that direction is no doubt a difficult challenge. Imbalances in manpower generation and manpower requirement are attempted to be kept to a minimum, for which forecasting of future industrial society, nature of industries, jobs therein, is very important.

(d) Making educational complexes attractive enough, to young and old, so that the entire society becomes a continuously learning society.

(e) Finances required for technical education are increasing from time to time. To mobilise the required financial resources especially in a scarcity situation, like in India, is yet another challenge. But more difficult than that is how to make effective utilisation of available finance.

Solutions to Meet the Challenges

(a) *The Solutions lie in expansion and deversification of technical education facilities*

Engineers are considered to be the primemovers, the engines for growth and development, of a nation without which the raw resources cannot be converted into usable goods and services, so essential for raising the standard of life. To catch up with the rest of the world and remain on the forefront in respect of technology, economy and politics, it is very essential to have a large number of engineers.

The recent trend that the technical education is going in private sector especially for meeting the growing education needs of society is a welcome sign. Newer ideas are being generated to make education more relevant responsive to local needs and yet cost effective. They are making a value addition in human resources at no cost to the Government, and hence they should be welcomed. Peoples participation, enthusiasms in this cause needs to be shaped well.

Producing engineers in only conventional branches like Civil, Mechanical and Electrical is not enough. There are vast employment generation and economic development opportunities in the fields, such as electronics, ship building, space technology, atomic energy, oceanography, bio-technology, natural energy resources, computer technology, transportation, etc. which need to be harvested for which technical education reaching to excellence is the need of the hour. Thus, technical education and training be oriented towards newer sectors rather than traditional disciplines.

The entire world is a job market for the highly educated youth. The mobility of personnel who have received graduate and post-graduate education, world over, is very high. Availability of job should therefore not pose any problem. Career engineers in fact create jobs.

(b) ***Financial allocation and Resource generation is essential to meet people ever growing demands on technical education***

Technical Education is not a concern of the Government only. It is a concern of everybody including industry, voluntary agencies, co-operative organisations, philanthropic bodies and individuals. Financial assistance for Technical education on priority basis has to come from all the beneficiaries, in varying proportions depending upon local conditions.

The experience in Maharashtra and other Southern States in mobilising financial resources through involvement of Society has proved to be fairly successful.

If technical education is more important than Arts and Commerce education, should it be allotted priority for grant-in-aid, is a important question which the Government should answer. If it applied the principle of modern financial management technique, namely "Zero Based Budgeting" the answer is obvious.

(c) *New organisation pattern for imparting technical education is very essential for newer objectives*

The problems of technical education development are becoming increasingly complex. The conventional organisational pattern which has served well in the past, because of the changed situation, is no more fit. Setting up of Technological Universities so as to justify and lay proper thrust on development of technological skills in the society is being increasingly realised Government of Maharashtra and other States have already initiated steps in this direction. It, however, needs to be pushed through early for the good of all.

So as to anticipate technological changes and the emerging technological skills, it is necessary to set up a cell in every state which should function like a search light and scan the technology horizon to foresee in advance the requirement of facility to be installed at the technological institutes and Universities. It should provide guidance to all the institutes in the State and will have well structured links with development plans of Central Government. State Government and the International agencies, such as UNESCO, UNDP, UNIDO, ILO and Universities in developed countries.

(d) *Expansion of Post-Graduate, Research and Consultancy Services in Institutes can create an appropriate culture for learning*

The rapid advances in Science and its technological application to meet stiff competition in trade and commerce at global level have demonstrated the importance of high level Engineering Education and Research.

Research and consultancy by the Universities and Colleges are the missing links at present for want of which both the industry and economy are put to great disadvantage. It may be desirable to deliberately lay a thrust on the establishment of Research and consultancy facilities at each degree level and Polytechnic level institute. They should have to undertake research projects including those for import substitution, from both private and public sector industrial organisations, and thereby also generate financial resources for their own updating.

Transfer of appropriate technology to the needy and vast masses, so as to improve productivity is possible to be achieved through this type of extension efforts. The systems and procedures will have to be redesigned so as to facilitate achievement of the above said object, including desisting significant incidence of brain, into the developed countries.

The industries which lack research facilities and atmosphere in the company may pay and create research faculty (chairs) and allied staff required and post them at the institute where research facilities exist.

(e) *Entrepreneurship development can help to harness the youth energies*

Developing entrepreneurship amongst the youths at various levels needs no emphasis. Technological capability, hard work, enthusiasm and finance etc. alone are not enough to set up and run an enterprise successfully. But for entrepreneurship training to our youths with vast technical knowledge are not able to grow to the level they are capable of and become self-employed. An entrepreneur has to have the knowledge and skills so that the remains innovative, creative, productive and becomes an asset to the society at large. These aspects have got vast potential for generation of employment and development of industries, especially in the backward areas and for backward communities. The Government have been designing various schemes through SICOM, MIDC, DSSIDC, DIC, Social Organisation, which however, due to paucity of entrepreneurial skills are not utilised to the full extent.

(f) *Up-gradation of quality of technical education can make youth capable enough to move world over*

Presently, the quality and standards of technical due to sudden and rapid expansion and diversification which is expected to continue also in future is far from desired. The institute campuses by and large are not so attractive and do not possess requisite harmonious academic culture. This invites immediate attention as follows:

(i) Technical teacher is the kingpin of the institute. He ought to be provided enough of opportunities for attending seminar, symposia, service training courses within the country and more so abroad by granting sebatical leave. Financial allocation and chalking of programmes in this regards is the pressing need. This kind of exposure to teachers will go a long way to improve education culture in our institutes.

(ii) Mobility of the teachers within the Government, aided and private institutes may be permitted.

(iii) Experienced personnel from Industries and other Government Departments should be encouraged to come in teaching by granting incentives, if necessary.

(iv) Establishment of State and National level awards for the teachers in technical education will build up their morale and create new culture congenial for better teaching and academic activities.

(v) Continuous renewal of the laboratory equipment and machinery commensurate with development of latest technologies demand immediate attention.

(vi) Licentive should be given to the teachers for writing books producing video films, textural materials and adoption of newer educational technologies.

(vii) The libraries at present are very dwarf. This results into lesser learning by the students. Attempts will have to be made to make the libraries attractive, real self-learning places and rich in technological books and journals from all countries.

(viii) Special efforts to continuously upgrade the quality of teachers, their pedagogic skills, work ethic, their involvement in institution building, social awareness and national development, are suggested. A scheme should be prepared to depute our teachers to developed countries on short-term basis, for two months or so. This will attract better talent in teaching, and improve work culture.

A institute at State level to do the education planning, revision of curriculum, reforms in examination systems, development of teaching material, design and conduct of short-term programmes for management and allied staff is also envisaged, with a view to qualitatively upgrade the performance of the system.

(g) *Training and placement in industries for rural youth would enhance their performance*

The institutes located in rural areas lack opportunities of training and placement because they are located away from training of all aspiring youth in industrial growth centres like Bombay, Pune, Nasik and Aurangabad etc. with necessary residential facilities may have to be strengthened. In industrially backward districts entrepreneural development centre/production oriented centres/ appropriate technology centre with close association with the academic institutes and nearby industries needs to be visualised. Linkages with surrounding National and International agencies in the subject on priority basis will have to be conceived.

(h) *Examination reforms can make them knowledge oriented*

Universities and Colleges legitimately occupy the role of a "Seat of learning". They should not turnout to be examination or registration bodies, as we see today. The tution classes on the other hand on self-finance and voluntary basis are assuming the role of real learning places. They have no powers, whatsoever, to examine and register the students yet they are crowded. The culture of learning has to be deliberately introduced in Colleges and Universities.

Many employees in private and public sector now conduct their own recruitment tests. During service also employees have to upgrade their knowledge, time and again, by attending courses. There is a continuous learning and continuous evaluation. As such the importance of degree examination, at every semester by the college level. University should not spend much time effort and money on examinations. It has to be incidental, internal. Autonomy to the institutes, in this regard more so to low standard institutes may be beneficial, so that they grow quickly and do not continue to remain inefficient under the umbrella of University.

(i) ***Cafeteria approach courses can establish better relevance with individual needs***

The University and Colleges possibly need to design courses on "CAFETERIA" approach.

A number of combinations of subjects with more relevant curricula and academic freedom need to be offered to the students. They may choose subjects according to their interests which is found to lead them to "excellence". It is a practice in many countries like U.K., Germany, U.S.A., etc. The system deserves to be given a fair trial.

This, however, does not mean that the present standard straight jacket courses should be stopped. It only means that many more options need to be provided to the students.

Now learning is a life long process, this is especially true because of fast changing technologies. Short-term intensive courses, correspondence course, television course, sandwich type course, self-study, in-service training course, evening course, day or block release course, could be developed using staff from technical institutes and industry utilising spare physical facilities during spare time.

Improving productivity in education is becoming the need of the hour. This is more so because the whole society is tending to become a learning society. This would require a large number of professors, institutes and financial resources, if we have to follow the existing educational technology.

Electronics T.V., Video films and such other media are likely to make change. This change should be welcomed and brought about quickly so that the quality of education goes up and the cost falls down to the level which the economy permits.

12

Report on 4th World Conference on Continuing Engineering Education

The Fourth World Conference on "Continuing Engineering Education" was organised by UNESCO in collaboration with the Peoples Republic of China at Beijing from May 17th to 19th, 1989.

More then 800 delegates for about 90 countries, developing and developed, participated. About one hundred papers on various aspects of "Continuing Engineering Education" were presented. The paper "Continuing Engineering Education of Teachers in India - New Approaches" written by Prof. B.B. Chopne, Prof. B.M. Naik and Mr. M.L.Waikar was presented by Prof. B.M. Naik on 19th May, 1989.

The policy paper of UNESCO on "Continuing Engineering Education" was presented by Dr. Ibukun. In his paper he projected high demands on Education of Engineers in 21st Century requiring the activity of "Continuing Engineering Education" in all the Countries. This has become very essential especially because of the New Challenge of Technology Revolution and its utilisation for well being of the human kind. With the increase in population of the World, and to cope with the rising aspirations of people. "Science and Technology" needs to be respected, developed and applied in various vocations and professions on increasing scale. Innovations in Science and Technology have to be encouraged and incentives be provided to science and Technology personnel for their outstanding contributions.

The potential of personnel qualified in Science and Technology, regardless of the boundaries of the Nations, need to be fully explored. Continuing Engineering Education plays a important role in this. Some of the important objectives of C. E. Education as outlined in the Conference are:

1. To increase National and World productivity.
2. To use latest Science and Technology.
3. To avoid sickness of Industries.
4. To respond to International competition.
5. To improve competence of working engineers.
6. To accept challenges and make best use of available opportunities.
7. To keep engineering talent upto date.
8. To promote innovation capacity of engineers.
9. To maintain life long competence.
10. For preparing engineers to shoulder responsibilities more ably.
11. Greater job satisfaction.
12. Change of job for betterment.
13. Learning new technologies.
14. Job growth and promotion.
15. Filling gap between formal education and practical industrial needs.
16. Avoiding obsolescence - Ensuring Employability.

Budget is being earmarked by UNESCO for undertaking C.E. Education Programmes all over the World. Project proposals are being invited from various countries, which would be scrutinised and funded by UNESCO. An International Association of C.E. Education with the objective of providing Continuing Engineering Education World over has been constituted with the headquarter in Helsinki (Finland). In the Conference various Countries have shares their experiences on C.E.E., latest situation of C.E.E. in a few countries is given below:

United State of America (U.S.A.)

In U.S.A. "Continuing Engineering Education" is quite an old hat. It is offered by many professional societies of engineers. It is also offered by Universities, most of whom have opened special departments exclusively for C.E.E. About 30 per cent students in Universities are C.E.E. students. C.E.E. is being further strengthened to maintain and develop superiority and Competitiveness of United State industry.

The need of Continuing Engineering Education is perceived by the engineers for their own growth, so also by their employing organisations. Universities find it a rewarding experience to run C.E. Education courses for they generate income besides obtaining interaction with industry for mutual benefits.

There is a committee appointed by United State Government to look into career long education. On its recommendation the United States Government have established accreditation Board to control quality of C. E. Education. It is realised that C. E. Education is very useful to increase National Productivity and develop intellectual capital resources.

University of Texas, Madison and several others have setup. CC TV. Uplink Antenna, Networking, Interactive video disks, PCs, Computer Aided instructions, etc. Cable Television, Microwave transmissions for C. E. Education is very important. Engineering Schools are widening their scope and working for professions besides teaching to students. They are now aiming at developing a continuously learning society. Which is believed to be the crucial development for human welfare.

China

In China the concept of "Continuing Engineering Education" was introduced from abroad around 1970. So far C.E. Education has played a important role in improving the performance of Industrial and adaptation of imported technologies etc. experience demonstrates that C.E. Education is the key to Science and Technology and economic development.

It has been the policy of Government to promote C.E. Education and have established many Institutes exclusively for the purpose. Every Ministry has formulated plans and programmes to train engineers. At the enterprise and institute level, plans have also been made for identification of objectives, contents, requirements and adopting scientific implementing measures for Continuing Engineering Education.

In 1981, Government made it a rule that each Science and Technology person must receive minimum one month training in 12 months period. It has now become a pre-requisite for promotion of professionals. C. E. Education in China is both a right and obligation of Science and Technology personnel. It is a constituent part of development plan of the department, and expenses incurred are regarded as production cost.

Various professional associations and societies have also played important promotional role for ex. China Association of Science and Technology (AST), China Association of C. E. Education (CACEE). It arranged International level Continuing Engineering Education programmes for top executives, especially in Collaboration with UNESCO.

They have prepared a grand master plan using satellite, TV, Audio, Video, PCs, etc. for Continuing Engineering Education.

The two major difficulties they experience are -

(a) Shortage of good Professors,

(b) Education material.

China is considering to make a low on Continuing Engineering Education so that the large organisations pay for themselves and Government to pay for small organisations.

Quality Teaching material constitutes the basic guarantee for the success of C.E. Education is their experience.

West Indies

They lay more emphasis on use of satellite in Continuing Engineering Education. University of West Indies is using satellite from 1978 to cater to 14 territories. They regularly arrange interactive video conferences, symposia via satellite. Faculty of engineering of the University has played a pivotal role in establishing the centre.

Traditional methods of C.E. Education have many limitations the same are overcome in this method. However, there is a inherent danger in this method viz. of lack of quality control on education. By careful planning errors can be kept to minimum if not eliminated. These methods are more cost effective. It requires a sound organisation and good faculty to prepare lessons.

Satellite has a large impact in education, with satellite telecommiting, one will be able to attend International Conferences at one's own place. It is very inexpensive method, and is making a beginning of a new era in education. Potential is being exploited on priority basis to extend it to wider areas.

In Japan, "Continuing Engineering Education" enjoys not only support from top management but also leadership and active participation in the conduct of programmes. They believe that employing people without education and training is a mistake on the part of management. Employee Education starts with the start of an organisation. They consciously attempt to develop self-supporting and challenging individuals with the ability to cope with the changing environment and technology by self-initiative and self-learning. In many companies the basic philosophy is, company is only as good as its people. The foundation for company development lies in development of its people, such that they work with joy and pride.

The training consists of modules such as Administrative, Economic, Political and Technological systems. Emphasis is laid on hi-tech as Computers, Microprocessors, robotics. Universities and associations of industries take a leading role in imparting Continuing Engineering Education.

It is a firm contention that Continuing Engineering Education is connected with research. An University or Engineering School can be effective in C. E. Education, if it has a faculty group that keeps pace with the rate of technological development. Continuing Engineering Education is not a additional burden for colleges. It is instead an important factor to bring about self-development and reform in education. The interaction opens up new areas for research and raises the level of teaching and scientific research. Continuing Engineering Education helps teachers to convert their knowledge into productive force, and raise their influence over the profession. From the Society and Nation point of view it provides a chance to combine theory with practice, which is so essential to advance the professional practices.

The most serious task in this is the development of R&D manpower. After development with so much effort it is likely to be under utilised.

An observation in Korea is that 83 per cent of Ph.Ds are in Universities having access to only 10 per cent of resources and 10 per cent of Ph.Ds in industry having access to 60 per cent resources. Academic and R&D manpower is grossly under-utilised in Korea. Continuing Engineering Education has resulted in Korea from ambitions plans for industrialisation, and continuous dialogue between industry and institutes. Furthering of C.E. Education demands a passion on the part of teachers to teach and rewards to those who receive C.E. Education. Without incentives C.E. Education becomes difficult.

In many Counties like China, USA, etc. satellite is found to have a large impact on education. Automation in education is the new trend in which Computer Aided Teaching (CAT) occupies a prominent place. The new technological development requires new advanced methods of transferring education.

In many socialistic countries like USSR, Poland C.E. Education is considered both an obligation and right of an employee. An employee must undergo C.E. Education when deputed. When not deputed he can as a matter of right ask for opportunities for education.

In West Germany, "Continuing Engineering Education" is considered to be an investment and insurance for better future. It is believed that the College or University Education can only react to fundamental new developments with a time lag. Usually several years elapse between introduction of new technologies and their inclusion in curriculum of teaching institutes. The aim of engineering course is to produce graduates fit for employment not that they are necessarily fully trained. Introduction of advanced technologies in industry demand C.E. Education for qualified employees. It is the contention that, at present the greatest barrier to the implementation of technological innovations is the lack of qualified employees. In other words, organisations do not find suitably qualified personnel on the labour market and pressure of time hardly allows them to train them themselves. In future, the updating of qualifications must be one of the factors taken into consideration when planning the introduction of new technologies.

Big Companies in West Germany spend on education of their employees. While with the small companies such measures go unrecognised or are undervalued. Their experience is that company run courses are more effective which have high standard, independent and are practice oriented. New technologies create new needs of C.E. Education is well recognised in West Germany. It is possible to learn in a course new things which would take perhaps years to learn from work in a company. They teach to forget the traditional ways of thinking and promote new ways which are untried as yet.

The paper presented by Prof. B.M. Naik was very well received. The conclusion of the paper that Continuing Education of Engineering Teachers stands as foremost in developing Countries like India and that International Cooperation, Exchange of Professors and support from UNESCO in the form of fellowship needs to be increased. In the absence of well competent Professors in Engineering Colleges, not only the students remain inadequately educated but the whole Engineering Society lends to remain less competitive by global standard C.E. Education tends to remain less effective. The efforts being made to train teachers under ISTE and QIP Programmes were very well appreciated. In conclusion, in India and especially in Maharashtra it is necessary to build partnership between Institutes of Technical education and Industry for the overall growth of both of them. Technologies employed in PWD, MSEB, State Transport Corporation and other State and Private Industries is requiring modernisation. According to a latest survey the productivity of men in India 1/29th of Japan, 1/10th of China and 1/8th of Korea. The share of India's export in World market has dropped down from 2.33 per cent in 1947 to 0.4 per cent in 1989, largely on account of lack of technological capability by world standards. A scheme must therefore specially be drawnout to open C.E. Education Departments in every Engineering College. A seminar or meeting of key persons of our department and industries may be organised to welcome the innovative ideas for implementation of C.E. Education.

The New Education Policy of the Government of India (1986) has also emphasised the need of starting "Continuing Engineering Education" centres to begin with in selected colleges. It has recommended establishment of Regional Resource Development Centres for "Continuing Engineering Education" to develop learning resources, which would keep linkages with Indira Gandhi Open University, New Delhi. Advisory Committees for each cluster or sector of Industry are also proposed by New Education Policy.

Retraining Employees
If I had 8 hours to chop a tree I would spend 6 hours sharpening my axe.

WHY APPRENTICESHIP?

In the complex world of today, jobs are not as simple as they used to be. The advances in science and technology are having a great impact on the working life of a man. He may be a farmer, weaver, or a businessman. He has to know now much more of his trade than his forfathers knew. His work is changed greatly by electricity and machines. With the growing industrialisation new jobs and skills, quite large in number, have come in existence.

In earlier days when a person had learned a trade he could practice that trade throughout his life. Today, because of the sudden explosion of knowledge and fast-advancing science and technology, trade practice undergoes rapid changes, and as a result the worker has to have the ability to relearn the trade during his service career. The kinds of tools and appliances which workman has to use are now much complicated and diversified. The extent of job intelligence he has to have now is much larger than before. He needs to have sound basic knowledge so that at subsequent stages he does not require much time to learn new techniques and skills. Physical work is gradually reduced and intellectual work going up.

The day-to-day living is also highly influenced by technology. To be able to derive really good benefits from the science and technology for better work and better living, it becomes necessary that the labour force is educated and trained to possess multiple skills. A variety of skills makes it easy for employers to adopt new processes and technology for production without any problem for employees on that account.

In view of the above, the traditional method of training the craftsman does not suffice. Picking up skills through observation is no longer enough. We need to teach youths as quickly as possible with the least expenditure of material and effort to the needs of a job, with the potential ability to up-date the trade skills. With the fast growing population and higher expectations in the standard of living, it is further necessary to make the learning as economical as possible.

Methods of Training

In the traditional method, children learned the trades at the hands of their father of master craftsman. This was mainly practical training. It was hardly accompanied by any systematic theoretical instruction. As a result, the trainees did not get a broad idea of the process as a whole.

The skills that used to be transferred to youths were lesser than the skill of the master craftsmen. Skills were thus gradually getting reduced from generation to generation.

With the advent of science and technology it became necessary to educate craftsmen in theory subjects also knowledge became important alongwith practical experience. Thus, arose the system of training youths in schools in theory as well as practicals. This removed the deficiency of theoretical content. However, the practical training in a school workshop lagged behing as compared to the old method. It is quite understandable because the workshop of a school can at best imitate the atmosphere of a factory. The speed of work and accuracy of jobs can hardly be developed in a school workshop in the same way as in a factory production shop. Moreover, in this time of rapidly changing technology new machines are being installed in factories. All such machines cannot be installed in school workshops.

Apprenticeship education and training provides both theoretical and practical training. An apprentice works in a realistic work situation. He learns on latest models of machines in the real environment of work in production shops. This is supplemented by theoretical training in classroom. It is not a mere training of muscles. It is a training to equip young people with knowledge, skill, intelligence and morale.

Through the apprenticeship scheme, youths contribute to the national production right from the stage of learning. By avoiding wastage of materials and rejection of products, apprenticeship helps to reduce hidden losses.

When persons are systematically trained as in apprenticeship, they become more capable of absorbing modern science and technology in their occupations. They become a little more innovative and inquisitive. This in turn leads to improving the performance and productivity, thereby reducing the cost of products and raising the standard of living.

Because of the stipend paid to an apprentice the burden on his parents is reduced to that extent. The cost of training to the State is very much less as compared to training is a school and college. Since he turns out products, the stipend paid to an apprentice is not a burden on industry either. In our country where the population of youths is quite large, such an economical method of apprenticeship is indeed most wanted.

An apprentice starts earning money from the day he is engaged. After the learning of the trade his earning power gets further increased. This makes him feel more and more secure and optimistic in life. This improves his social attitude. He becomes proud of his trade, and develops zeal for it. Thus, apprenticeship is also an agency which stabilises the society by stabilising the individual.

Humanistic Aim

Kerschen Steiner, a German educationist, said at the beginning of the century that occupational or vocational education stands as the first and foremost thing in making a man fit to lead a life worthy of a human being. When a young boy or girl learns a trade, he or she learns not only the trade technique and skill but, perhaps more important, also learns to see the problems of living and develops the ability to solve them. This training brings about a sort of mental and spiritual development of the person that he can identify himself in the context of the changing social, economical, political and technological scene in the world.

Spranger, another educationist, also emphasised the same point and added at Apprenticeship should not be viewed merely as an agency to supply skilled men to industry. Men are not to be viewed as machines designed to do work. The humanistic aim of making them fit men and women in this world is the ultimate aim, and teaching them to do work is a milestone in that direction.

Objectives of Apprenticeship Act, 1961

The Apprenticeship Act, 1961 has declared the industries or workshops in the country as training shops. They are no doubt the production shops, but recognised places of learning like Universities and Colleges. Apprenticeship Act, 1961 has been passed following broad objectives:

1. To organsie on a systematic basis the training of apprentices in industry with a view to meeting the increasing demand for skilled craftsman.
2. To utilise fully the facilites available with industry for training of apprentices.
3. To ensure the training of apprentices in accordance with programmes, standards and syllabi drawn by expert bodies.

An evaluation of the statutory Apprenticeship programme, conducted by the Maharashtra Government and reported in January 1977, bears out all that has been stated above. In this study it is indicated that apprenticeship is very popular and very well received by both the industries and apprentices, and that it possesses high potential to ease the national problem of employment and training.

The act has been further ammended in 1973 to cover the apprentices of degree and diploma levels. The apprentices are given stipend at prescribed rates. It is obligatory, as per act, for the company to take a member of apprentices as prescribed by the apprenticeship adviser.

MANAGEMENT EDUCATION FOR INSERVICE ENGINEERS

Science and technology is advancing at a much faster rate than at any previous time. There has been a mushrooming of scientific fundings in the last two decades, and new dimensions to professional and management skills have become open. As a consequence, demands made on engineering personnel, especially because of the launching of five-year plans, have greatly changed. The development plans, programmes and projects are characterised by super size, complexity, uncertainties, new technology, and involvement of multiple agencies, besides frequent political interference in their implementation. However, the engineering personnel in charge of these are often not equipped in terms of the necessary managerial skills. As a result, the physical and financial resources are not optimally utilised and hence full value of their potential benefits does not become available for human welfare.

The existing system of management education is inadequate in terms of both quality and quantity. Management education is a decisive factor for economic, social and technological development of a country. It is, therefore, of vital importance to review the existing system and tailor it to suit the requirements of today and possibly those of tomorrow.

Objectives of Engineering Profession

Engineering profession has certain obligations to the society-continuing services to improve the living and working conditions, devising ways and means to effect savings in efforts and materials, safety to society, etc. The forefronts of basic sciences are continually advancing and opening new areas for engineering endeavour. An engineer has to be alert to assimilate and translate advances in science into engineering practice. Thus, engineering is far from static and is essentially a creative profession.

However, accomplishing this with only technological capability without possessing necessary management skills is a difficult task. There are a large number of obstacles of social, cultural and political nature which present serious problems. These are experienced right from policy level upto day-to-day working. An engineer, therefore, has to have capability to negotiate and get along well with them, use them in favour if possible, avoid if not, and find way through a hurdle race. Raising capabilities of engineering personal to tackle the situations, and to make most of the national resources for the welfare of the people, is the present need. Management education for inservice engineers has therefore to prepare men to be fully competent to do the professional practice without fear, frustration and failure. Further, engineering and management education should inspire every engineer with necessary spirit to enable him to deal with new situations on his own initiative and confidence. He should develop a desire and sense of involvement for taking an active part in changing things in the profession. In India, organisations are undergoing drastic changes. New organisation structures, relationships, delegation of authority, responsibility, in view of ambitious development plans are being formed. This can take a proper shape only if engineering executives are thinking in terms of shaping them rightly rather than merely accepting what is offered. An inservice engineer has, therefore, to be able identify himself in the context of changing society, organisation, economy, technology play an active role. Further, he should be able to think of a right approach to attack, evaluate and test the results at each stage.

Why Management Education?

It is said, 'India is a rich country, but inhabitated by poor people'. India is rich in terms of natural resources like land, water, minerals, etc. but their utilisation is poor. Although India has the third largest technical manpower, because of the lack of the management capability it remains one of the less developed countries have been spending large sums of money on establishing projects like irrigation, power, dairy, etc. However, largely due to inefficient management they are not coming up as they should. They suffer from delays and cost overruns. The break-even point gets so prolonged so much so that at times it becomes out of sight and goes beyound the maximum production capacity. As a result even before the project is commissioned, it becomes 'non-starter' and project is commissioned, it becomes 'non-starter' and sick. In India, about 20 per cent of the sick industries are reported to be in this category.

Often the payback period gets prolonged. Before a project has paid back its capital investment due to fast changing technology, it becomes obsolete and is rendered sick. About 20 per cent of sick industries are reported to belong to this category. Poor management is seen also in production and operation stages. As a result utilisation of the already installed capacity in industries, land and water of irrigation projects, etc. is very low. Due to variety of reasons in manufacturing industry, capacity utilisation is reported to be only 74.4 per cent, whereas in agrobased industries it is hardly 42 per cent. In the other hand, capacity utilisation of the multinational organisations operating in India, in the same environment, is more than 100 per cent. The only point of difference between the multinationals and the Indian companies is management competancy. On account of management deficiencies, Indian industries have been working with almost outdated machinery, retaining large inventories, inefficient manpower and adopting inefficient systems and procedure. Most of the technical personnel management who are holding managerial positions today, have picked up management knowledge only by observation. Very few of them had a systematic education in management science. As a result, no wonder they operate at less efficiency than what they are capable of. The loss due to not educating engineering personnel in management, therefore, is very high. If it is done properly it is found to increase the effectiveness of the application of technology facilitating rapid spread of the research findings to the remote rural areas. If the benefits of technology are to be carried to common man swiftly, an engineer needs to be trained properly to manage the same. Above all management education is essential to enable an engineer to make most of his potential abilities.

Existing System and its Deficiencies

Management education in India is of relatively recent origin. It received impetus in the sixties when the management institutes at Calcutta and Ahmedabad were set up. When the products of these institutes were well received, many universities followed by opening management departments, offering courses in business administration. Because of popular demand, some of them have started part-time courses for serving people. One interesting feature is that most of the students studying management are having engineering background.

The Government of India has also been conducting since 1976, a large number of management development programmes for officers in Government and Public sector corporations. This is with a view to induct new management knowledge for improvement of performance of public sector. National Productivity Council has been conducting similar courses for private sectors. Besides, many organisations have their own in company programmes.

In spite of all these ongoing efforts it is found that the training facility, both qualitywise and quantitywise, is very inadequate. The national level seminars and symposia held recently have recommended that there is an urgent need for upgrading the training effort cadre in public sector corporations. Government is considering the same,and planning to put up a National Academy for Management Studies.

One common deficiency observed in the MBA programmes of universities and management institutes is that the courses represent borrowed models from the developed countries and as a result, there is a lack of fit. They are oriented more to industrial enterprises and profit making organisations whereas, in a developing country like India, these courses ought, in addition, cater to agricultural and rural developments. The social, cultural, economic and political factors are the crucial variables to be attended to by the development and managers and administrators. The management courses are highly deficient in these subjects. Therefore, although large sums of money and effort are spent, yet there is much scope to improve. The various elements of the system such as training institutes, faculty, physical facilities, training material, training needs and above all organisational environment need examination.

Sometimes short-term training programmes are cancelled for want of participants. Sometimes irrelevant courses are also offered. Faculty of required subjects and level is not available because the pay structure is poor. Some feel that receiving training is of no use, because what is taught is too theoretical and due to political and vested interests it cannot be practised. As a result, organisations consider it a waste of time and do not depute their people for training. Some programmes are held in five star hotels, and the Universities, the seats of learnings, sit silent.

Reforms Needed

Employers and employees in India by and large are not yet sold to the idea of life long education. The walls between learning and working still hold tight. Therefore, more effort and incentives are needed in both private and public sectors to make the concept of continuing education more popular and acceptable. Since developing management capabilities of engineering personnel is important from national point of view, perhaps it should be made obligatory to the employers to provide enough of the opportunities to their employees especially in young age, to continue education and develop to the level they can. This means that employers should draw out a plan for the development of personnel. At least two persons per year need to be deputed liberally at national and international levels to attend the programmes which may be offered in modules, such as, finance, personnel, operations research, material, marketing, etc. Government should encourage this by providing some financial incentives like rebate in income tax, etc. Employers in turn should grant special benefits to those who attend and acquire proficiency, pass examinations and publish articles. Maharashtra State Electricity Board, a public sector undertaking with a view to develop professional culture, grants advanced increments to those who pass MBA examinations. This trend should, however, multiply. Simultaneously, need is felt to improve the quality of management education suited to the needs of the country. In developing countries like India, MBA programmes and other short-term management courses, unlike the similar courses in developed countries, should lay emphasis apart from profitability, on social and economic developments. The focus of management courses ought to shift from maximisation of profit to maximisation of human welfare. In the pursuit of profit, unscrupulous entrepreneurs otherwise do harm to the society by rendering the industries sick.

Participation of political and social leaders in the organisation of the programmes is likely to improve the position. Since, political interference in developing countries is increasing, introducing this new trend could be given a fair trial. Improvement in the working of institutions offering such courses naturally follows. Then only they will be able to attract the professionals for training and continue to do so. Good faculty members is the first prerequisite. In the absence of proper pay scales, however, it becomes very difficult to retain them. Facilities for faculty development by way of exchange programmes between the countries are found to be rewarding. It is practised in some institutions. There is, however, a greater need to enlarge these.

Engineering colleges, professional institutes like the Institution of Engineers (India) and universities need to equip themselves to open continuing education centres and extend to professionals their physical and academic base. A look at the structural formulation and functioning of universities and colleges is, it is felt, urgently necessary. The University of Roorkee and a few Institutes of technology have set up such centres and their experience is encouraging. A determined effort on the part of the Government is necessary to transplant this culture of continuing education in rest of the institutes.

13

Overview of Continuing Engineering Education in India

Continuing Engineering Education

The college is recognised by the Government of India as a centre for CEE. It regularly conducts a number of courses for both teachers and engineering personnel in industry.

The mix of industry people and teachers is desirable, because then there is a lot of exchange of ideas during the classes and also outside the classes. A residential course is better, becuase it gives them more chance to interact. To enable the engineers to keep changing and remain flexible they ought to have such chances for learning.

As an example the college has conducted the following courses for both industry people and teachers:

(1) Microprocessor Applications (two weeks).

(2) Safety for industry (one week).

(3) Industry Institute Partnership (two weeks).

National Scenario

The concept of continuing education has had a long history in India. The department for CEE at the University of Roorkee has been working more than fifty years. However, CEE has not yet become "Peoples movement". There are several efforts made by various organisations. The Indian Institutes of Technology conduct regular courses leading to M.Tech. and Ph.D. There are also short-term quality improvement programmes on important topics for faculty and practising engineers. The duration of these kinds of programmes varies from one day to a few weeks.

Big industries have their own training centers including State Big Industries department such as State of Maharashtra's MERI (Maharashtra Enginering Research Institute). Nasik etc. Administrative College, Institution of Engineers (India) and The National Productivity Concil of India.

Even at Universities there are Staff Training Colleges Indira Gandhi National Open University daily telecasts educational programmes through the national network. There is a Council for Technical Education which provides guidance and financial support to institutes and industry for the CEE in the counrty.

Various seminars, workships and conferences are also conducted at national and international levels by various organisations.

Indian Society for Continuing Engineering Education

Professor B.M. Naik, Principal and Mr. A.K. Rajurkar have done very important work for the founder office at the Indian Society for Continuing Engineering Education whose headquarters are situated in Roorkee University.

A National Conference as held in October 1991 by the department of continuing education of University of Roorkee.

India-Canada Project

The Government of Canada and India have signed a M.O.U. in 1991 to participate in the programmes of continuing and non-formal education. The project is founded by the Canadian International Development Agency. The project has transformed 12 polytechnics into more resourceful institutes. Each institute is now offering a large number of CEE programmes helping the development of their surrounding areas.

Survey

Professor B.M. Naik and Mr. A.K. Rajurkar have conducted a survey in a nearby area, through a welll structured questionnaire. One of the most important findings was that awareness of the need of CEE among the practising engineers is increasing, but they are still dependent on their employer to take the financial burden.

Other Important Findings

1. Though the importance of CEE is realised, employees don't attend it whole heartedly and perhaps that's Why Employers Don't Depute Their Staff to it Liberally.
2. One of the reasons the courses offered by the institutes do not match with the people's needs.
3. Universities do not play an active role.
4. There is not much previous experience available.
5. Prevailing rules of security of job and promotion reduce the needs of CEE.
6. Courses based on research work are more successful.

TRAINING AND DEVELOPMENT OF ENGINEERING PROFESSORS: NEW APPROACHES

The potentials of engineering teachers professors are said to be high, which for want of proper training and exposure to global competition remain untapped and even underutilised. Consequently, the technical education imparted to students in spite of huge effort, time and money spent is not only inadequate, but is also misdirected. No wonder, if the promise from Indian engineers and industry is also not fulfilled and available opportunities in international and domestic market lost. India's position in export market in 1984 has dropped down to 42nd. Although in terms of rupees exports are increasing, but in percentage of export trade in world it is consistently dropping down. Proper development of professors is important, not only for themselves, but more for students, industry, and the nation at large.

A professor assumes the role of a kingpin in the process of techno-economic development. If he falls short of the requirements, the whole system of education and economy gets damaged. The productivity of engineering education, returns from physical and financial resources allotted to laboratories, buildings, library, industry, etc. for want of proper opportunities of development of professors remain low. Countries like Hong Kong, China, Japan, etc., which have achieved fast economic growth have invested in education and educators greatly.

The input required for training of educators as compared to capital investment in buildings, equipments, etc. is far too low while the value addition because of high multiplying factor is too great. It is, therefore, argued that we have to learn to invest more in development of our educators.

Training and development of a professor is not only the training of an individual to teach technical subject in a narrow sense but it is much beyond that. It is more helping him to develop to the level he is capable for, and to enable him to apply theory to professional practices to raise them to successively newer heights. An engineering professor has rightfully to be a leader in technology and not merely a follower. Engineering professors in our institutes therefore, be allowed, encouraged and helped to enable them to grow to the level of their counterparts in developed world. This has to be the revised target of training and development of our present day professors. What is the role of Government, Institutions and Professors themselves is analysed in the following.

Essentials of a Professor

A professor in an engineering college/university worthy of the post is expected to lay an impact on the practising professionals. He ought to be involved in teaching and research. Indian universities so far have neglected research and have become only teaching bodies, which is damaging so remarked Prof. S. Chandrashekar Nobel Laurate during his visit to India in 1984. Professor should also be able to connect his research with industry and to market it.

Technical knowledge is now the real capital, and latest of it ought to be possessed by a professor. He must also have attitude and ability to apply his knowledge for regional development and welfare of the community.

Previously, the technical institutes were on the periphery of the process of development, now they have come to its centre. They are the major source of technical knowledge to improve productivity, 85 per cent of national economic growth of U. S. A., and 88 per cent of the employment generation is attributed to technological innovation. The worthy professors are now termed as engines of growth and generators for innovative ideas. The demands on the engineering professors are:

(a) to impart professional education to vast masses, economically and effectively,
(b) to retrain labour and inservice engineers in emerging technologies on continuing basis. About 40 per cent of the students in U.S.A. are mid career students while with us they are only 0.05 per cent,
(c) to provide new commercial ideas and technical talent to industry,
(d) to help to develop new industries and generate new jobs which is badly needed,
(e) to provide techno-economic information and advice to various development agencies,
(f) to participate actively in modernisation of industry and import/export of technology.

Role of Government and Present Status of Training and Development

Government pervades modern society. It has always been central to the process of development in general and industrialisation in particular. Preparation of infrastructure like technical manpower is crucial amongst its responsibilities. It has obligations to develop the engineering educators matching with its industrialisation plans. A balanced investment has to be made in technological education and physical assets of industry. Recognising the importance of faculty development in New Education Policy (1986) Government has strengthened following schemes:

(i) ***Quality Improvement Programmes (QIP)***

These are inservice programmes formulated for upgrading the quality of personnel in engineering colleges. The programmes are covering regular M.Tech. and Ph.D. courses. Institutes like I.I.T.'s R.E.C.'s and some engineering colleges are offering courses under QIP programmes.

(ii) *Indian Society of Technical Education (ISTE) Programmes*

With an objective of advancing the cause of technical education at various levels (namely degree, diploma, etc.) the ISTE sponsors short-term courses, conferences, seminars and symposia in the area of engineering education, methodology, subjects, curricula and management of technical education. This is a major activity for upgradation of teaching skills.

(iii) *Programmes Sponsored by Professional Societies*

There are a large number of professional societies to various disciplines of engineering and technologies institution of Engineers (INDIA), National Productivity Council. Computer Society of India are leading amongst them.

(iv) *Short Comings*

The major short comings are as under:

(a) *Exposure to international scenario*—The various courses conducted by ISTE and other professional organisations are good. But they do not expose him to training in developed countries like U. K., U. S. A., Japan, etc. As a result the professor in our country does not know the role played by his counterpart in other countries.

Any amount of lecturing in this respect is not a substitute to doing by hands. They would be much more motivated, if they are exposed to global scenario.

Professors are best developed, if they are allowed to rub shoulders with collaborators from foreing countries. There are more than 13000 foreign collaborations in India. Most of the deals are signed by administrators. There is hardly any transfer of technology through these deals. Only import of equimpent takes place. The training component in these deals is not utilised to the full extent. The Indian companies are reported to be interested by and large in only profit, production and not in technology. Conscious efforts need therefore be made by Government to involve professors in the import of technology. This will provide them an opprtunity to develop to world standards.

(b) *Lack of Research Grants and Marketing Orientation*—Experience in the world tells us that, researching is the best method of learning, which unfortunately due to lack of research grants from Government is not available to most of the teachers in engineering colleges. As a result the professors growth is stifled and crippled.

Most of the research grants are presently given by Government to CSIR labs, where the research is done mostly by Science graduates.

Some professors who do research, often it remains in laboratories and journals. It takes a long lead time, if at all, used in industry. Skills and structural organisations of marketing are conspicuously absent, which ought to be developed through conscious efforts.

(c) *Lack of Programmes to Promote Skills for Book Writing and Video Film Making*—Most of the books in engineering subjects are imported very few books are written by Indian authors. It is a high time that our professors are provided facilities to develop skills of book writing, video film making. It is not only for saving foreign exchange, but it is more for writing need based books and developing capability.

There is a beautiful scope to export books to less developed countries, and those opportunities are also lost for want of in capacity of our professors. If they cannot write books, cannot publish articles, it means that by world standard they are small and need to be developed.

(d) *Lack of Seminars*—The training courses are effective for Junior Teachers but for senior teachers seminars are found to be more effective. Such research seminars be specially arranged in every branch of engineering so that competition and excellence could be promoted. However, the grants required for organisation/seminars are not available, as a result development of professors in on reduced scale.

14

Need for Technical University

In order to become a significant economic power in the 21st century, it is essential to restructure the Indian engineering education without further loss of time and integrate the same with indigenous research alongwith horizontal expansion of industry. The rapid changes in technological scenario, faster development of newer technologies alongwith their judicious applications in industry demand a fresh look of traditional organisational structure of colleges and universities. The age-old methods, structures, linkages and values which served well at one point of time, are nowadays totally outdated and no more relevant in today's context. Strategic restructure, as well as reorganisation of technical education by establishing more and more technical universities, is the pressing need of time. In this paper, it is reiterated that without revitalising the technical education by establishing technical universities, Indian economy and industry, howsoever desired, cannot grow and .become globally competitive. Reforms in technical education should precede the industrial reforms.

Present Requirement

For various reasons the existing universities in India have failed to cope up with the demands for fast changing technological scenario. Though the country possesses a massive infrastructural base in technical education consisting of a large chain of engineering colleges, vast pool of teachers and students, but it has not been so responsive to changing needs due to its inherent weaknesses, universities have been thwarting, impeding these colleges and people in them. They are 'Hamstrung' organisations unfit for nursing new ideas and technologies. They are far behind their counterparts in developed nations.

Though a large number of graduate engineers and technicians come out from Indian universities every year, yet the scientific and technological achievements of the country bear no relation to these vast numbers of S&T personnel. The quality, as well as relevance of education by world standards, is somehow missing today.

The need of the day is to undertake massive programmes to educate masses and encourage innovations to country's need so as to provide a new direction to Indian economy and business. This cannot be achieved through the conventional universities, because of the simple fact that they are incapable of facing these challenges. It requires exclusive treatment like agricultural universities which integrate education, research and extension.

In liberalised economy, external pressures are mounting on Indian industry forcing them to restructure so as to become competitive. The industries which cannot cope up with this change would become sick, and ultimately go out of business. It is seen that multinational companies in India are absorbing latest technologies and recruiting competent manpower from outside. So as to equip Indian Industry with able manpower and also to be competitive in future, it is imperative that the curriculum of technical education be changed without further loss of time to meet the future requirement in this vital area.

Huge investments are made by both public and private sectors towards the industrial development. But because of inadequacies in technical education and consequently less flexibility in engineers, they are less productive. Most of the industries are sick locking up huge capital in them. The productivity of industry now depends largely on the performance of personnel. The human resources produced by these institutes are the input to Indian industry and hence their capability is of vital importance to industry. Unless this manpower is globally competitive, the industry cannot prosper.

Research Base to Education

Today technical education institutes are, suffering from the deficiency of innovations. Many of these institutes have no research departments. Without proper avenue of research base, engineering education cannot grow and become up-to-date. It is seen that the basic premise of technology changes four to five times during the entire service career of a teacher. A teacher cannot teach the latest developments in the field of his specialisation, if he is not exposed to the latest developments. Technical education institutes now in changed situation have to provide not only competent manpower but also newer technologies to industry.

To cater to these needs, technical education institutes should be restructured. It is found that students learn best by doing research and hence, a strong research base to education institute is imperative.

The foreign collaborators have brought newer plans, products and processes to Indian industry. The educational institutes and academicians in India have remained away from industry.

On the other hand, collaborators have gone closer to them. Time has come that industry and institute should bridge the gap and develop a system which would revitalise both the parts on a continuing basis.

Path Shown by Agricultural Universities

Agricultural education, research and their application in India are looked after by the Ministry of Agriculture, Government of India, which is primarily responsible for growth and development of agricultural production. The agricultural universities (set up after 1960) in various states receive their financial grant from the Ministry of Agriculture, and not from the Ministry of Education, Government of India. The directions and targets for education, research, etc. are also monitored by this Ministry which provides matching grants too.

It is believed that this strategy has been the basis of India's success in alleviating its food problem, increasing food production (from 50 million tonnes to nearly 200 million tonnes). Had the agricultural education continued to be governed by the Ministry of Education, it would have never received the priority, funding and direction that it needed to address the nation's critical problems of food crisis.

To increase the industrial production substantially, it is necessary to integrate the higher education with industry. It seems appropriate to bring higher education and industry in the same ministry.

This strategy of putting engineering education, research and industry under one ministerial roof, is especially applicable to developing countries where industrial development plans may be going in the direction while technical education and research plans are going in another, as if one strategy has nothing to do with the other. As a result, there is much irrelevance in education and research.

It is seen that many engineers and educated people are unemployed on the one hand, while people possessing required skills and knowledge are rarely available on the other. Huge capital investments in industry remain idle or underutilised making the industry unstable and allowing them to perform well below their installed capacities.

Allocation of fund to industry, education and research is important, but more important is the productivity of funding. Fund productivities would yield better result provided higher education and industry are strategically coupled.

Universities and education ministry, especially in developing countries, tend to be insensitive to market opportunities. They are ill equipped to understand and cope up with the high-speed environment of business. *Universities sometimes have a lack of vision in relation to the speed and direction of industrial growth. They continue to work on more traditional lines forgetting the need for the student's community as well as industrial sectors.* If teachers continue to teach what they know rather than what students ought to be taught, then the whole exercise of higher education becomes meaningless.

Therefore, a structural reform in funding mechanism as well as strategic control of industries and institutes is urgently required. If appropriate sectors of education and industry are brought under the same ministry, there will be a better coordination. This hypothesis has been tested in the agricultural sector yielding a positive response and, therefore, it is desired that such a trial be made in the area of engineering education also.

Michael Porter in his book, "Competitive Advantage of Nations" has observed, from comparative study of ten nations, that nations are industrially advanced where there are more technical universities. Secondly, Technical Universities are more productive, cost effective, than comprehensive Universities.

Suggestions

Lateral expansion of technical education coupled with a strong research base alongwith judicious application of fruits of scientific developments be considered necessary in integrated manner while setting up a technical universities.

Following suggestions be considered:

- One of the Government colleges in each region be elevated to the university level which would not only avoid unnecessary delay but also simultaneously reduce cost.
- Degree, diploma institutes and ITI in a region be brought under the control of a technical university, regardless whether these are private/aided or Government funded and steps be initiated to make them autonomous.
- Technical education be clubbed with the Ministry of Industry, Government of India, in the line of agriculture universities. This idea has already been recommended by UNESCO especially for developing countries.
- A council of leaders both in industry and in education be set up at the state level to look after planning and monitoring of technical education.
- Industrial services department, innovation centre, and technology park be set up at each university, so as to provide 'Technology Push' to economy and to reduce sickness in industrial sector.

A CASE FOR INITIATIVES IN TECHNOLOGY TRANSFER

Learning from the experience of other countries it can be said that Technology Transfer and Marketing from Higher Technical Education Institutes to Industry and *vice versa* is the pressing need of Indian economy. Japan's multinational enterprises have, for long, established links for Technology Transfer and Research and Development (R&D) not only with institutes in Japan but also with institutes in United States, United Kingdom and Europe. This is considered to be one of the important factors which has enabled Japan to become an industrial leader. In India, this far, it is more the foreign collaborators who have propelled the industrial growth. Academicians and Technical Education Institutes have remained away from industry. Now time has come when they should stop working in isolation and move towards each other.

Technology Transfer has become a major phenomenon in global economy. It is being considered a key to industrial competitiveness. Technology Generation, Dissemination, Patenting, Intellectual Property Rights, are some of the current important issues before the nations.

Technology level of a nation has become the determinant of its economic wellbeing. Therefore, efficient organisation and management of technology transfer in any nation more so in India, is the need of the hour. Performance of institutions dealing in technology in isolation, ought to be discouraged. Fresh initiatives to integrate the working of universities, CSIR labs, engineering colleges, industrial estate, chamber of commerce, on the lines followed in Germany need to be introduced forthwith.

True that India is relatively a late starter in industry. It has traditionally been an agriculture based country. However, the Government now has taken a policy decision to build India a technology oriented nation and things are moving fast in this direction. Many engineering colleges have come up, especially in southern states, and more than 1,00,000 engineers are passing out each year. Industrial Estates are being established even in small towns.

There is an atmosphere of enthusiasm in commerce, trade and industry. There exists a market pull which badly needs a Technology Push, which the higher education institutes ought to give.

Although essential, mere development of technology in laboratories and dissemination through usual methods of education, training, publication is not enough. The new technologies need to be transferred quickly and efficiently to industry to increase their productivity. Effective partnership between academics and industry in technology transfer is found to revitalise both the industry and the institute. They both thrive on each other's support. Today, in India there exists no technology transfer department in most of the academic and research institutes. However, the consciousness to set up such department is increasing. Technology transfer, usually known as Extension, exists only in Agricultural Universities in India.

Engineering Colleges as Technology Providers

Engineering Colleges, IITs, Polytechnics, which so far remained away from industry have recognised that they have to bring about industrial development also. They have a leading role to play in innovation and entrepreneurship. So far the foreign collaborators have been transferring technology to Indian industry. They will kept doing so in future. But it is more expensive and makes us dependent, the Ministries of Industry, Commerce, Trade and Education have to consider worldwide developments like Technology Parks, Incubators, Entrepreneurship Centres and adopt them with modifications, if necessary, to suit our conditions. Japan and Germany have set up such institutes on the periphery of technical education institutes. Why can we not do that? Can our institutes not serve as a hub for area development?

Higher Education Institutes and Industrial Estates

A large scale programme is undertaken by Central and State Governments to set up industrial estates and growth centres. Large investments are being made in them to provide infrastructure like land, water, electricity, etc. Huge amounts of loans and subsidies, are being given to entrepreneurs in backward areas. Young enthusiastic persons are taking up to entrepreneurship, working hard day and night with a dream to become industrialists. However, many of these enterprises in the course of time become sick. Some entreprises are born sick due to wrong conception, some choose wrong technology and their future in spite of big market and hard work, is not bright.

The academic institutes, colleges, IITs and CSIR labs should show concern as to why many industries become sick. What could be done to avoid this? The Government would have to dovetail the role of knowledge organisations, technical organisations with the establishment and running of industrial estates. With the increasing role of technology, the existing systems and procedures of industrial estates will have to be altered, it is not enough to have money and raw material to run an industry. Appropriate technology has assumed great importance. It is also not enough to have monitoring cells for industries in banks which give loans. Technology Audit has now assumed more importance than financial audit. There are doctors with various specialisations to cure patients. Similarly, multiple approach to cure industrial sickness has become necessary.

Shall we, in India, not transfer this organisation invention to our industrial estates? As the maternity homes are necessary for safe childbirth, so are the incubators and science parks for safe start of companies.

We do have a few of them. But they are so few that in a big country like ours they hardly make their presence felt. The government has a central role in bringing together, the industrial estates and innovators. U.K. has implemented "Teaching Company Scheme" and European Commission has implemented "COMET" to improve competency of existing workforce in industries. Cost was shared by industry and government. Can such schemes improve the performance of Indian industry and reduce sickness? The benefits are far more than the cost.

Venture Capital

Venture capital has been playing a vital role in promoting/starting of new technology based firms in developed countries. In India government companies like RCTC, TDICI have made a beginning. But there are no private venture companies. The experience reported is, that the funds instead of being used for new untested technology, are being used by big companies for routine purposes. Will the VCF companies reach the innovators? This is going to decide the innovation and growth. A change in direction of usage of VCF is desirable. Academicians have to come forward to use them and to test their new ideas and products.

International Co-operation

In the present time characterised by globalisation, UNESCO and similar bodies have a crucial role to play. They ought to facilitate developing countries, to learn New Technology, without being required to reinvent the wheel. In India, there exists a market pull and technology push is wanted.

INNOVATION AND TECHNOLOGY TRANSFER PRACTICES AND POLICIES IN GERMANY: LESSONS OF EXPERIENCE

Need and Importance of Technology Transfer

Technology Transfer (TT) has become a major phenomenon in global economy. It is being considered as key to industrial competitiveness. Technology generation, dissemination, patenting, licensing from Higher Technical Education Institutes to industry, especially small and medium scale enterprises are some of the current issues before the nations. Technology level has become the key determinant of a nation's economic well being. Therefore, efficient organisation and management of technology transfer, technology development in any nation, more so in India, where there are ambitious plans of industrialisation, technical education and research, is the need of the hour.

Merely development of technology in laboratories and dissemination through usual methods of education, training, publication is not enough, although essential. The new technologies need to be transferred quickly, efficiently to industry to increase their productivity. Effective partnership between academics and industry in technology transfer is found to revitalise both the industry and institute. They both thrive on each others support.

Today, in India, there exists no technology transfer department in most of the academic and research institutes. However, the consciousness to set up such department is increasing. Technology transfer, usually known as Extensive, however, exists only in Agriculture Universities in India.

The aim of this survey and study is therefore to draw lessons of experience from Germany and identify models which could be adopted in Indian environment to build a healthy and regenerative relationship between its industry and technical education institutes.

About Survey Methodology

The survey was not an exhaustive study, carefully developed and systematically administered, with carefully selected sample of respondents. Rather it was based on interviews of scientists, professors, administrators and students working at several German Research Organisations, Universities, Polytechnics, Industry, etc. Most of the respondents were from Karlsruhe region and a few were from Berlin, Stuttgart, Hamburg and Braunshweig. The interviews and discussions were conducted by the author himself. The author visited 3 research labs, 6 universities, 4 innovation centres, 2 polytechnics, 5 companies and 2 chambers of commerce. Many Professors, Scientists, Technology Transfer Officers, Students and Administrators were interviewed in sufficient depth, so that their responses contribute to the study. Whenever possible, interviews were arranged with officials who would have broad perspectives and experiences. Some of the professors and scientists had visited India and had knowledge about the Indian Institutes and Industry. One of them was Dr. Engleman who worked in India for ten years in Indo- German Co-operation project. Factual data regarding the size of programmes, amount spent, number of licenses etc. were not readily available from many respondents and hence not used.

Some obvious themes and trends emerged from this study. They would be very useful to Engineering Colleges, Polytechnics, and other research institutes, which are contemplating to work in research besides teaching and be a major player in regional development. The way technology transfer is organised, supported and carried out in Germany, in an integrated manner by Research Laboratories, Universities, Polytechnics, Innovation Centres, Technology Parks, Steinbeis Centres and Chamber of Commerce have many positive aspects.

Positive Aspects

German Government, both federal and .State, have taken a positive view and support research at national laboratories, Universities, in-house research in Industry, Polytechnics, Chamber of Commerce, etc. and installed organizations to transfer research findings to industry, to develop new products and processes, so as to maintain Germany as a leading player in world economy. The Government has sanctioned significant financial resources of about 3 per cent of GDP and human resources and put at the disposal of research institutes in both the public and private sectors. Government believes in "Public good" through applied research leading to new products, processes and techniques. Such innovations although at the cost of public resources are no doubt of significant value to the private companies or industry, but they also ultimately benefit the consumers and people at large. Innovation is the key to progress and prosperity, so is understood by common man. *They believe that those who innovate will lead, and those who do not will lag behind.* It is this attitude and respect for scientific research which is reflected in funding scientific institutions and other actions to promote research and its transfer to society.

The European commission with headquarters in Brussels has also been laying emphasis an R&D and technology transfer for maintaining competitiveness of European industry. They have .devised a number of programmes like Erasmus, Esprit, COMETT Leonhardo-da-vinci for research education, training in new technology, and to avoid technological obsolescence. Germany being a member country has been also implementing a number of projects funded by European commission in various Universities and Laboratories.

It will thus be seen that there is a full support from top i.e. Government of Germany, and European Commission of technology transfer which is a positive factor.

Multiple Approaches

The activities of technology transfer are conducted by multiple organisations which work in a network and not in isolation. The industry interacts with appropriate organisations, one of more depending upon the type of industry, level of technology and field of specialisation. The various organisations in Karlsruhe Technology region are depicted in the form of diagram as shown in Figure No. 14.1 which shows various agencies, and their connections with each other.

It will be seen from the figure that there are various agencies generating and transferring technology to industry. All these agencies function in an integrated manner. They are mutually supportive to each other, and also competing. This is the second positive aspect of German system.

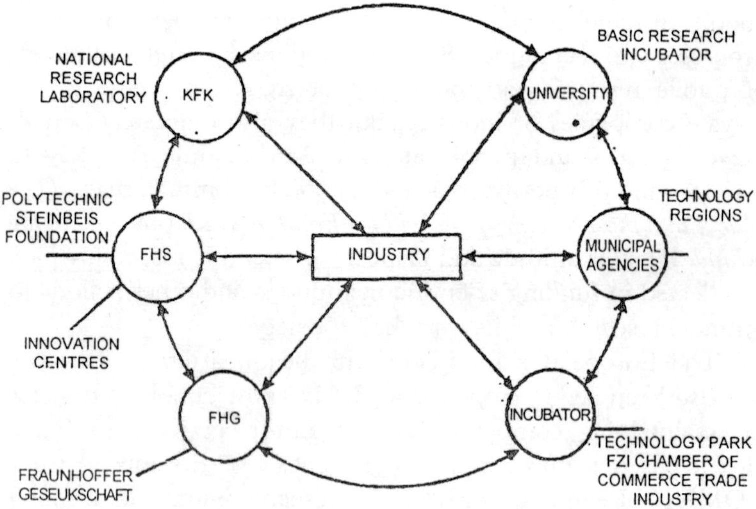

Fig. 14.1: Various agencies in Technology region Karlsruhe and their connections with each other.

The University and national laboratories largely involve in basic research while, Steinbeis Centres, Innovation Centres, Incubator and FHG involve more in applied research. Big companies are found by and large to interact with national laboratories, university and FHG, while small and medium interact more with Steinbeis, Incubator, and research companies like FZI exclusively set up on the region. There is however, no hard and fast rule. It may appear that there is duplication of effort, many organisations doing the same work. But it is purposefully designed to be so to develop a competitive spirit among themselves, and avoid monopoly.

University Technology Transfer Offices

There are 88 universities with science and technology discipline in Germany. Majority funding to Universities is from State Government. About 20 per cent come from Central Government especially for capital investment like construction of buildings, equipment, etc.

States have been active on technology transfer and have created technology transfer offices in most of the Universities. In Baden Wurtemberg State with a population of 1,02,34,000, there are nine Universities in which 2,21,000 students study, of which about 1,05,000 are in Science and Engineering. At University of Karlsruhe there is in addition an Intellectual Property Right (IPR) and licensing office providing service to all nine Universities.

The first of such offices was set up in the late seventies. In each office there are 7 to 10 persons, consisting of technical experts and supporting staff.

The mission of this office is to maintain industrial liaison, assessment of regional needs for new technologies and management of University outreach to the commercial sector by doing four activities, which are as under:

(a) *IPR and licensing* - The office consults and supports members of Universities with a view to improve commercial exploitation of scientific research results. It offers:

- Confidential consulting to faculty in all questions relating to intellectual Property Right applications.

- Financial support of IPR applications.
- commercial exploitation of inventions.
- IPR searches in international and national data bases.

(b) ***Fairs and exhibitions*** - Inventions, new projects and all services offered by University are presented in fairs like Hannover, to inform about the latest results in science and research.

(c) ***Research funding*** - It facilitates obtaining funds from public and private sources, like European Commission to various faculty.

(d) ***Advanced education and training*** - it offers to companies information concerning continuing education programmes to upgrade the competency of working engineers, scientists, etc.

There is a history of positive working relationship between individual professor and industry. Most of the professors coming from industry at middle age obviously relate research and teaching best to the needs of industry. Some of them while working as professors in University, work as honorary Directors in national or private research laboratories, and some of them have their own business. This enables them to find training places for students in industry and also jobs for outgoing students. The system is commended well by student respondent, University administrators, and professors. This relationship between professors and business has been at the back of good technology transfer in Germany. It provides professors an opportunity to do consulting in an industry relevant to their scientific expertise, and to receive a steady flow of real world research projects, topics for graduate and doctorate students, alongwith funds.

Till recently it was assumed that inventions would be completed to the market needs only in company laboratory, seeds of which however would be shown in University laboratory. Now with global pressure on competitiveness, University are taking projects to completion up to patenting and licensing. The trend of University staff is towards seeing the fruits of application of research findings in industry. It is believed that there is a greater charm for researcher to make new discoveries, but his pleasure is heightened when he sees that they have a direct application to practical life.

University as Incubator

The technology transfer office is maintaining close links with the innovators working in the University. The University is providing infrastructure to innovators to develop and carry out work on new ideas. One such case is of Dr. Sauter in Mechanical Engineering which deserves mention.

Dr. Sauter has done his Ph.D. on finite element method application to optimisation. He continued further research with a view to commercialise it, using University equipment, which he was permitted. Three more staff jointed him. Now he has developed software, which has won prizes. He has also registered his own company and is planning to shift to innovation centre. He spoke very high about the role of TT office and the University which helped him in crystallising his project into an innovative venture. He however, expressed about difficulties in obtaining loans from banks which insist on security. The venture capital fund scheme is not so developed in Germany.

Similarly, in machine design department, it is noticed that the department does lot of technology transfer to companies like Diemler Benz, Bosch, through students project work, contract research, etc. they have obtained seven patents and many innovative projects in association with TT office. With the coming of Korea in market for I.C. engineers it was told that German companies have become alert and contracting research more and more to his department.

There are many more cases of this type in University departments like chemical, electronics, civil, etc.

Technology Innovation Centre (Incubator)

This is a scheme from regional Government. It was introduced in the year 1984, and today there are more than 170 centres in operation in Germany. The scheme is meant for hi-Tech entrepreneurs, who have new ideas opportunities. The space and infrastructure are given on low rent, so that the entrepreneurs can concentrate more on their project ideas, rather than infrastructure development.

One such centre "Technologies Fabrik" is in Karlsruhe located adjacent to the University it is managed and maintained by the Chamber of Commerce. There are about 10 persons looking after the operation of centre. The entrepreneurs are provided here central facilities like Fax, parking, meeting room besides space on low rent. They are also given management and technical advice on demand. Presently there are 45 enterprises inside, and many are wanting to move into additional buildings which are under construction. The enterprises develop technology here and move out in a period of about 5 years.

It is reported by Dr. Stephen, Manager of the Chamber of Commerce that the scheme is very successful. The factors which contribute to success include nearness to University. The entrepreneurs are in close contact with the University for technical support. Many of the entrepreneurs are graduates from this University.

The Manager of the Technologies Fabrik mentioned that there is a pool of scientists and knowledge workers in Karlsruhe who would like to have space in incubators. After five years he said the enterprises have no difficulty in moving out, for at that time their requirement of space is much more, and the rent in fifth year as per agreement between them is also high. Management and control of incubator is with one agency namely the Chamber of Commerce. This is the other factor contributing to success. Berlin centre is found to be the best and other centres have varying degree of success depanding upon leadership quality of the person incharge. This scheme is implemented in many countries and deserves to be implemented in India and other developing countries.

The author has visited three enterprises in the Technology Fabrik. All of them have expressed full satisfaction for having company in the Fabrik. They are getting more recognition by being in one place, and their image is brighter than if they were any where else.

They see no difficulty in shifting from this place after 5-6 years. Till then they are nursed well and need no more support from this fabric.

Similar units known as "Technology Park" were visited by the author in Braunshweig, Harburg, and Berlin. Braunshweig University has taken a lead in establishing the park adjacent to its premises. About 100 companies are functioning in this park in the buildings owned by University. It has been set up in the year 1984 and since then many companies have taken birth in this Technology Park, grown well and migrated to industrial estates. Such companies maintain links with the University professors and researchers.

The park of Harburg is also an offshoot of the Technical University Harburg. This park has a huge premises of about 100 acres and three buildings. With the increasing demand for space in this park, the authorities have undertaken expansion. Harburg is relatively less industrialised area. The Technical University of Harburg has been set up 15 years before alongwith the Technology Park with the aim of developing the area. It has been successful, so remarked the President of the University.

At Berlin, an authority known as WISTA has been set up after Unification of Germany to develop east part of Berlin. This authority has taken up establishment of Technology Park and Hombolt University in this area. Already incubator of Environment Technology and Electronics are completed. There are hundreds of companies in them. The programme is very ambitions aiming at transforming the economy completely. The M. D. of WISTA who has come from industry, is very optimistic about the success. This project deserves to be emulated in India.

The Fraunhofer Institute for Systemtechnick and Innovations Vorschungs Karlsruhe have done and evaluation of this scheme in Germany. They have reported that there are about 170 centres in the country and they are doing a good work. They have added value to the industrialisation and improved income and employment. The regional economy by virtue of such centres has improved. The centes are further being expanded.

Steinbeis Technology Transfer Centre

This is a scheme initiated by Baden Wurtemberg State in 1983 through its Ministry of Science and Technology. It is to function as a problem solver clearing house for SMEs, utilising the existing strong network of R & D Institutions, Universities as well as individual professors and experts. Its winning strategy has been total identification with individual enterprises, tight formulation of projects which address their problems, rigorous search through its data base.

Today there are 220 centres, with about 3500 experts (full time and part time) doing service to 15274 enterprises. Most of the centres are based at technical colleges.

The underlying principle being to obtain intensive co-operation between academic, commercial and Govt. Institutions. It makes use of existing research infrastructure in FHS, University and other institutions. They have a financial independence but they must work as profit centres, and not as cost centres.

The author has visited six of them in Karlsruhe in the areas of computer, refrigeration, electronics and found them working successfully. The heads of centres are professors, employing 5 - 20 employees on full time basis. Students are also employed for whom this work is counted as project. The scheme gives a valuable feed back to professors, who in turn do more research or learn more and teach better in classes.

Institute for Innovation and Transfer

It is an innovation centre setup in the polytechnic of Karlsruhe, as per the scheme of State Government it is operated in 25 other centres in the State. The unit has a head and fifteen other employees. They do only research and no teaching. The research is done mostly on projects given by companies on payment. The IIT earns the salary of 15 employees through contract research.

IIT makes full utilisation of polytechinc infrastructure. Besides, it has some equipment purchased by itself in contract resarch projects on grants received from State 11 Professors of the FHS are also working in this centre, for which they do not get extra money but a reduction in work load. Those who work in Steinbeis Technology Transfer Centres as consultants, get feed back from industry, and to cope with industry assignments engage themselves in research in IIT, which is interdisciplinary.

IIT conducts Seminars on research done and participates in fair at Hannover. Presently 9 projects are in hand of which 2 are of long-term nature.

Dr. Link the head, said the success of scheme depends on the ability of the leader.

Forschungs Zentrum Informatic (FZI)

It is a Private Limited Company, an offshoot of the University of Karlsruhe, in the areas of Information Technology. It was started in University and remained there for 1½ years and then moved to its own premises which is adjacent to University. It is supported by the State Government.

The Company undertakes research contracts in the area of I.T. It employs 120 researchers on full time and 250 on part time. Six professors of the University are honorary research directors. It has thus close links with the University and derives its strength from it. Many students and staff work in this company on part time basis.

It has competitors like Steinbeis Centres, FhG Lab, and other companies. This is a good model worth emulation in India.

Forschungszentrum Karlsruhe (FZK)

It is a very big research laboratory, employing about 4000 persons of whom about 1000 are scientists. The institute is financed by Government. It is involved in fundamental research, but also undertakes contract research.

The laboratory has Technology Transfer and Marketing department in which to persons work. Dr. Just is the head. This office has granted hundreds of license of technologies to private companies, FZK provides licenses and also training to personnel who are using licenses. SMEs normally do not go to FZK, it is only the big hi-tech companies who go for licensing of FZK.

The Lab has very close links with the University. A few professors from Karlsruhe and other Universities work here as head of research departments. Many Ph.D. and Diploma students visit his lab for project work.

This is a unique feature of German system bringing about integration of Universities and Research Laboratories. It is missing in India and deserves emulation.

Fraunhofer Society

The Fraunhofer Society for promotion of applied research (Fraunhofer-Goselischaff-FhG) was founded in 1949 to "pursue research and development in the spheres of natural sciences and engineering on behalf of Industry",. FhG maintains 36 research labs at various locations in Germany, one of which is in Karlsruhe, covered in the survey. FhG has a staff of 5000, of whom 1500 are scientists and engineers. About 30 per cent budget comes form Government, (90 per cent from central, 10 per cent State), the balance 70 per cent is earned through contract research sponsored by agencies of the federal Government, the state and by private industry. Over the past ten years, industry sponsored project research has been the major growth factor for the society, while basic support from Government as a percentage has decreased from 45 to 30, the total FhG budget increased almost two times.

Expansion of Grant funds through Federal Ministry for Research and Technology (BMFT - Bundes Ministerium Fur Forschung and Technology) for projects that jointly involve industry and academics for Market oriented technologies.

Applied research is supported by Federal Government principally through BMFT, and to a lesser extent, through Ministries. Approximately 40 per cent BMFT's grants go to applied research and collaborative projects in research areas of high economic priority, known as Market oriented technology promotion. Such projects are implemented in co-operation with many Universities.

Recommendations

In India, there are Indian Institutes of Technology (6), Council of Scientific and Industrial Research Laboratories (30), Regional Engineering Colleges (17) and about 250 Universities, which engage in education and research. Only a few of them have in the recent past, (from 1990) started Technology Teransfer foundations/offices. There are 12 Science and Technology Parks and six incubators installed at the initiation of the Department of Science and Technology, Government of India. The schemes are however going slow. Universities and Engineering Colleges do not have Technology Transfer Departments. However, all the Agriculture Universities have Extension Departments, carrying technology from Lab to land.

Most of the Engineering Colleges (about 400) are like Fachhoch - Schule which are teaching oriented and have very little research. About half are in private and the other half in public sector. There are over 1200 polytechnics, which offer 3 years' course and they are also teaching oriented.

Industries in India, (SMEs) traditionally do not do research. They mostly make more profit by improving marketing, management and saving on taxes and importing technology, innovation in technology by and large is not seen as a means of increasing profit.

Many industries are sick for various reasons. Many industries depend on foreign collaboration for diversification and progress rather than on any academic or research institution within the country. It can be said that it is more the foreign collaborators who have propelled the industrial growth.

It is, however, increasingly realised in free liberal world economy, by younger generation that partnership between industry, research and technical education institutes is necessary. It is increasingly being viewed as an effective means for revitalising both, it is the need of the time that this complementary relationship between institutes and industry be achieved for which the following recommendations are made :

1. The Indian economy and industry are suffering from a deficiency of "Innovation and Technology Teransfer". To make up the same it is recommended that a committee consisting of experts from industry and academics under the Chairmanship of a industrialist be set up by Government. The Committee should prepare an action plan for implementation.
2. It is necessary to integrate the efforts of technology transfer between CSIR labs. Universities, Engineering Colleges, Polytechnic, etc. Government of India, considering the trends in world, should design a scheme for exchange of personnel, with incentives like in Germany that the professors have to have two hats,

one in university and the other in laboratory. This will improve productivity of research expenditure. Professors should be permitted to go in CSIR labs, IITs and industry. So also industry people should be invited as adjunct professors in institutes.

3. Set up technology transfer offices in each college, polytechnic, university. Today, not many institutes have such offices. Improved methods of technology transfer like licensing, patenting, consultancy, will have to be introduced, if we have to go with the world.
4. More funding from Government for R & D and Technology Transfer is badly needed. The Government would have to look financial figures of R & D in other countries, like USA, Germany and Japan. Today, it is spending around 1 per cent only and that too mostly in public sector. Productivity of R & D expenditure in public sector is lower than in private sector, and therefore a joint project, market oriented will have to be thought of by the Government of India and State Government. We may have to reconsider the industrial policy to promote R & D in Engineering Colleges and not only in CSIR labs. Today no R & D money comes to college, and youths are not provided access to research. This will have to be revised to build India as a technological nation.
5. ***Research Companies Private Limited like FZI:*** Set up private companies like FZI on the periphery of Universities and engineering colleges. The model of FZI in Karlsruhe is worth emulation. Committees may be appointed to prepare project reports with a view to propagate hi-tech and to provide opportunities to talented people within the country, organisations like this are necessary. This will help to avoid brain drain. It will build indigenous capability in hi-tech and make imports reduced.

   The leading Engineering Colleges and Universities should step in this area, so as to make application of high tech at a faster rate. The highly educated persons in subjects otherwise find it difficult to get chance to use their knowledge and they tend to migrate elsewhere. Such companies would help Universities to bring about regional development.

Alumni of the institute may be involved in setting up of such companies, by taking shares. The case of Wisconsin Alumni Research Foundation which gives grants to University for research and obtains patents on research findings, licenses the patents to COS and earns income which is put back into research is a good model like FZI.

6. *Establish Incubators*: Innovation centres adjacent to the higher education institutes like technologic fabrik in Karlsruhe.

The various state Governments are implementing ambitious plans of industrial development. They are spending through agencies like Maharashtra Industrial Development Corporation huge amounts on establishing Industrial Estates, in large, small and medium size towns. They are providing infrastructure in the form of land, water, roads and electricity. When the scheme was prepared there was no scheme like incubator. But now MIDC scheme would have to be redrafted in the light of such new schemes.

A look at the enterprises in the industrial estates indicates that many of them are sick for various reasons. One of the important reasons is that the technology they have chosen is not proper, it is less productive, when more productive ones are available. Now it is not enough to have money, raw material and market to run an enterprise. Proper technology is very important.

It is proposed that 'incubator' also called as 'Nursery for industries' to provide proper technologies as a part of MIDC scheme. As is maternity home necessary for safe child birth, so is a incubator necessary for healthy start up of companies.

Government should design a scheme of incubators for various areas out of industrial development budget. It will increase success of industrial estates. Now that VCF is available, in India, the chances of success are greatly enhanced. VCF without incubators weakens the scheme of VCF. Like Karlsruhe University, the Institutes have to extend their infrastructure to innovators, and the whole institutes function like an incubator.

7. ***Start Scheme like Steinbeis:*** The Steinbeis foundation of Germany has signed as agreement with C.I.I. for the implementation of the scheme in India. This is reported in Business India dt. 14-8-1995. This is a good sign.

   C.I.I. has thousands of member industries in the county. A message form C.I.I. to industries to tap expertise of Engineering Colleges. Polytechnics, is very important. It is a forward step to develop "Market Pull".

   New it is for the institutes to participate and cope up with the requirement of industries in respect of new technologies. The technical education department, Government of India, should whole heartedly cooperate, equip its staff and labs to a great extent.

   The scheme empowers the professors and avoids bureaucracy. The scheme should have:

   - Exchange of personnel-visit to Germany for 2-3 weeks for about 100 key people form academics, industry and Government.
   - Private colleges may be involved first who would be more devoted and flexible.
   - Exchange of students should be included in this scheme.

8. *Reform system of Higher Education* : Presently, professors have no research grants. The labs are not equipped. Research programmes for scholars should be started forthwith leading to Ph.D.

   Professors must also exert more to obtain research grants from industry, DOE, C-DOT, DST, etc. They would have to prove worthness and attract grants from industry be appointed as professors. Research would have to be stepped up greatly in Colleges, for without research there is no value for these institutes, and no patenting, licensing etc. If professors miss this in early young age, they miss it forever and remain professors by title and not by work. No doubt professors would have to be provided adequate incentives, like in Germany, freedom to work, research, to do private practice, etc. Research assistants posts be created on full pay to attract best talent of scholars. ISTE should play a vital role in establishing the rights and privileges of professors in India.

9. *Last but not the least* - Develop awareness for Market pull amongst industries and Technology push amongst institutes by conducting seminars and conferences jointly for industry and academic personnel. One sided effort by only industry or by only institutes is not enough. Both have to move to each other, for which it is recommended that academicians in association with Confederation of India Industry and similar bodies should organise seminars, and invite experts drilled in the minds of persons who matter most, without which it is difficult to build bridges between industry and academics.